The SPECIAL BLESSINGS PRAYER

Books By Donna Partow

Becoming the Woman I Want To Be: A 90-Day Journey to Renewing Spirit Soul & Body

Becoming the Woman God Wants Me To Be: A 90-Day Guide to Living the Proverbs 31 Life

This Isn't the Life I Signed Up For…But I'm Finding Hope & Healing

DONNA PARTOW

The SPECIAL BLESSINGS PRAYER

WEU Press
Ponte Vedra Beach, FL

ISBN: 9781731057518

Cover photo of Koro Sun Resort, Fiji by Suzanne Temming
Editor : Linda Harris

All scripture quotations, unless otherwise indicated, are taken from the Holy Bible, New International Version NIV.

Scripture quotations labeled KJV are from the King James Version of the Bible.

DEDICATION

This book is dedicated to my daughters,
Leah and Taraneh.
My two greatest blessings.

CONTENTS

A Gift For You

You are about to read a book about unleashing Special Blessings! What better way to get started than with a special blessing? So I'd like to give you a gift. It's a powerful video presentation on "The 3 Tests You Must Pass to Step into Your Destiny." You'll also receive a workbook for taking notes and an ebook edition of the teaching.

I know it will be a blessing to you. Just visit: www.specialblessingsprayer.com/gift to claim your gift.

If I can pray for you, stop by my Facebook Page to share your request.

Love & Prayers,

~ Donna

THE SPECIAL BLESSINGS PRAYER

The Story of David, Nabal and Abigail

Now Samuel died, and all Israel assembled and mourned for him; and they buried him at his home in Ramah.

Then David moved down into the Desert of Maon. A certain man in Maon, who had property there at Carmel, was very wealthy. He had a thousand goats and three thousand sheep, which he was shearing in Carmel. His name was Nabal and his wife's name was Abigail. She was an intelligent and beautiful woman, but her husband, a Calebite, was surly and mean in his dealings.

While David was in the desert, he heard that Nabal was shearing sheep. So he sent ten young men and said to them, "Go up to Nabal at Carmel and greet him in my name. Say to him: 'Long life to you! Good health to you and your household! And good health to all that is yours!

"'Now I hear that it is sheep-shearing time. When your shepherds were with us, we did not mistreat them, and the whole time they were at Carmel nothing of theirs was missing. Ask your own servants and they will tell you. Therefore be favorable toward my young men, since we come at a festive time. Please give your servants and your son David whatever you can find for them.'"

When David's men arrived, they gave Nabal this message in David's name. Then they waited.

Nabal answered David's servants, "Who is this David? Who is this son of Jesse? Many servants are breaking away from their masters these days. Why should I take my bread and water, and the meat I have slaughtered for my shearers, and give it to men coming from who knows where?"

David's men turned around and went back. When they arrived, they reported every word. David said to his men, "Put on your swords!" So they put on their swords, and David put on his. About four hundred men went up with David, while two hundred stayed with the supplies.

One of the servants told Nabal's wife Abigail: "David sent messengers from the desert to give our master his greetings, but he hurled insults at them. Yet these men were very good to us. They did not mistreat us, and the whole time we were out in the fields near them nothing was missing. Night and day they were a wall around us all the time we were herding our sheep near them. Now think it over and see what you can do, because disaster is hanging over our master and his whole household. He is such a wicked man that no one can talk to him."

Abigail lost no time. She took two hundred loaves of bread, two skins of wine, five dressed sheep, five seahs of roasted grain, a hundred cakes of raisins and two hundred cakes of pressed figs, and loaded them on donkeys. Then she told her servants, "Go on ahead; I'll follow you." But she did not tell her husband Nabal.

As she came riding her donkey into a mountain ravine, there were David and his men descending toward her, and she met them. David had just said, "It's been useless—all my watching over this fellow's property in the desert so that nothing of his was missing. He has paid me back evil for good. May God deal with David, be it ever so severely, if by morning I leave alive one male of all who belong to him!"

When Abigail saw David, she quickly got off her donkey and bowed down before David with her face to the ground. She fell at his feet and said: "My lord, let the blame be on me alone. Please let your servant speak to you; hear what your servant has to say. May my lord pay no attention to that wicked man Nabal. He is just like his name—his name is Fool, and folly goes with him. But as for me, your servant, I did not see the men my master sent.

"Now since the LORD has kept you, my master, from bloodshed and from avenging yourself with your own hands, as surely as the LORD lives and as you live, may your enemies and all who intend to harm my master be like Nabal. And let this gift, which your servant has brought to my master, be given to the men who follow you.

"Please forgive your servant's offense, for the LORD will certainly make a lasting dynasty for my master, because he fights the LORD's battles. Let no wrongdoing be found in you as long as you live. Even though someone is pursuing you to take your life, the life of my master will be bound securely in the bundle of the living by the LORD your God. But the lives of your enemies he will hurl away as from the pocket of a sling. When the LORD has done for my master every good thing he promised concerning him and has appointed him leader over Israel, my master will not have on his conscience the staggering burden of needless bloodshed or of having avenged himself. And when the LORD has brought my master success, remember your servant."

David said to Abigail, "Praise be to the LORD, the God of Israel, who has sent you today to meet me. May you be blessed for your good judgment and for keeping me from bloodshed this day and from avenging myself with my own hands. Otherwise, as surely as the LORD, the God of Israel, lives, who has kept me from harming you, if you had not come quickly to meet me, not one male belonging to Nabal would have been left alive by daybreak."

Then David accepted from her hand what she had brought him and said, "Go home in peace. I have heard your words and granted your request."

When Abigail went to Nabal, he was in the house holding a banquet like that of a king. He was in high spirits and very drunk. So she told him nothing until daybreak. Then in the morning, when Nabal was sober, his wife told him all these things, and his heart failed him and he became like a stone. About ten days later, the LORD struck Nabal and he died.

When David heard that Nabal was dead, he said, "Praise be to the LORD, who has upheld my cause against Nabal for treating me with contempt. He has kept his servant from doing wrong and has brought Nabal's wrongdoing down on his own head."

Then David sent word to Abigail, asking her to become his wife. His servants went to Carmel and said to Abigail, "David has sent us to you to take you to become his wife."

She bowed down with her face to the ground and said, "Here is your maidservant, ready to serve you and wash the feet of my master's servants." Abigail quickly got on a donkey and, attended by her five maids, went with David's messengers and became his wife.

1 Samuel 25: 1-42

1. Introduction

What do you want?

That's a loaded question, right? But what do you really want? You want to love and be loved. You want relationships that are enjoyable, not filled with pain and confusion. You want your life to make sense and for circumstances to actually work *in your favor*, rather that feeling like the whole world is conspiring against you. And you want power to live what you believe and the ability to walk away from stupid habits and self-destructive behaviors. You wouldn't mind praying…and actually getting answers!

You want your life to *work*. You want to be, in a word, BLESSED.

That's a great word, by the way. It literally means not only happy but so happy everyone around you ought to be jealous of you. Seriously! When God says, "I'll bless you and make you a blessing," he's saying that he wants to write a story in your life that's so beautiful, so incredible, so unbelievable that everyone who hears about it *should be envious!* Imagine that.

But how do we step into that level of blessing? That place in God that is so immeasurably above anything we could ever ask or imagine, that people living ordinary lives are tempted to jealousy—which, sad to say, they will be...but that's a whole different book and not your problem. Love them and let them just *deal with it!*

This book is about you having the blessings of God chasing you down the street and overtaking you. It's about **The Special Blessings Prayer**—a prayer that will unleash God's love, favor and power upon your life in such measure, you won't be able to contain it all.

Who am I to be writing this book? A better question would probably be: *Where am I to be writing this book?* Because I'm sitting at the Koro Sun Resort and Rainforest Spa on the spectacular island of Vanua Levu, Fiji, where I've been living for the past two months. Yes, I'm living at a four-star resort where they filmed an episode of *The Bachelorette*. This is, without dispute, one of the most beautiful places on the face of the earth. If you're wondering exactly where it is, pick up a globe and look for "the middle of nowhere." That's pretty much where I am. (Hint: look around the South Pacific.)

The staff all know me by name, treat me like a princess and serve me gourmet meals when they're not busy scurrying up trees to pick me fresh coconuts. I bike along the ocean each morning, down the Hibiscus Highway (yes, it's named after the wall-to-wall flowers growing on either side). I always pick one and stick it in my hair for good measure. Then I read a devotional on my Kindle in a hammock, maybe go kayaking to look at electric-blue starfish, swim a few laps in the infinity pool overlooking the pristine blue-green ocean or just wander around in awe at the majesty of God's creation.

Right now, I'm sitting in their seaside restaurant, which is only open for me at the moment—for my exclusive use as an office to write this book, which is why I came to Fiji in the first place. I'm overlooking the Koro Sea, where I and a collection of small tropical islands are waiting together to greet yet another breathtaking sunset.

Go ahead. Take a moment to deal with that whole "to be envied" thing. I'll wait a second. If it makes you feel better—and it may or may not—my journey to this place has been a daunting one, filled with devastation, loss and humiliations galore. And those are the three I'm willing to mention on the opening pages. Maybe I'll get to the truly awful stuff later. I had to give up everything—especially my preposterous pride—and allow God to reduce me to absolutely nothing. I had to come to the infamous "end of myself" to discover the power of **The Special Blessings Prayer**.

It wasn't the way I thought it would be. And perhaps I've taken a more arduous path than necessary. I do have a track record of doing things the hard way, that's for sure. I strongly suspect you may have moments, as you read the coming pages, when you question the wisdom of this prayer and the process behind it. But I can promise you:

IT WORKS

The Special Blessings Prayer is not on trial. You're not my guinea pig. The process you are about to undertake will absolutely, positively change your life—if you fully participate. I know that because I've prayed it with hundreds of people with phenomenal results.

Are you ready to begin? It starts with a list.

2. Begin With Your Special Blessings List

Before you can pray **The Special Blessings Prayer**, you're going to need a list. And I bet I can guess what you're thinking! You're thinking this is going to be a list of all the things you want and the stuff you need God to give you or do for you. Or maybe you suspect I'm going to suggest making a list of the people you love or people in need, just to remind God to do something nice for those folks too. Typically, in church circles, that's called a prayer list.

Hey, how about a gratitude list? Those are great. Maybe start by counting all the blessings God has already showered on you, count those blessings, name them one by one and then God will pour out even *more* blessings on your already-grateful heart.

But no. That's not the kind of list you're going to need. My journey began with a list. And yours must begin there too.

Actually, my list began with a phone call so let's back up and I'll tell you about that. I was crying on the phone, again, with a pastor's wife I routinely turned to for prayer and counsel when ministry hurt. You don't need to reread the sentence, you didn't miss something—that's what I wrote: ministry hurt. In fact, after decades in ministry, I felt so beat up I began noticing little things like *women's ministry director* and *weapons of mass destruction* both have the initials WMD. And I had begun routinely referring to the process of working with church staff as "entering the belly of the beast."

Seriously. It was that bad.

I was telling my friend, the pastor's wife, that I'd been working hard to forgive all the people I felt had done me wrong—and I was actually sorta proud of how magnanimous I was being, given that none of them *deserved* or had even *asked for* my forgiveness. She interrupted my self-congratulations to inform me that forgiveness wasn't good enough. I had to do more than forgive; I had to proactively *bless* those who had hurt me.

Bless them? *Bless them?* I was proud of the fact that I hadn't gone all Jersey Girl on them and unleashed the full fury of what I *really* thought about how they'd treated me! And here she was implying that biting my tongue wasn't an epic feat of inner strength! *Bless them?* Well. That was just weird. Weird and dumb. Why on earth would I want God to bless *them?* I wanted God to bless *me* so all those people would see for themselves that God was on my side and they had gotten it all wrong. I wanted God to bless me and vindicate me and show them a thing or two about who God's favorite child was.

Then I made a fateful decision that might just change your life.

I decided to ask God what he thought of my friend's ludicrous suggestion. It turns out, he agreed with her. I don't remember everything he said, but for me it was one of those burning-bush/voice-from-heaven moments. After I hung up the phone, I walked into my prayer room, sat in my rocking chair and bowed my head. With tears streaming down my face, I asked him, "Why on earth should I ask you to *bless* people that I want you to *punish*? It's not what I want at all! I want you to make them pay for what they've done to me! I want them to realize how unfair they've been."

And the God of the universe reached down into that little prayer room, in the midst of my anguish, and began to lift the fog of confusion and pain left behind from years of trying to "figure everything out." I'll tell you much more about my encounter with God later in the book, but for now, the only words I'm ready to share with you are these:

whether or not

Right now, those words don't mean a thing to you and you probably think it's odd that I gave them so much white space in this book. But trust me—when the power of those words finally dawn on you, as they dawned on me that fateful day in my rocking chair, you might want to find a white wall in your house and just paint those words on it so you never forget them.

Back to that whole list thing.

I took out a notebook and made a list of everyone who had hurt me and who I was still holding a grudge against. For most normal people, that should be two different lists, the second one being much shorter than the first. But for me, they were one and the same. I nursed a grudge against every person who had ever hurt me. And some of the offenses were *so slight* as to be utterly absurd. In fact when I finally got honest, most of the hurts were more accurately described as *slights*.

These were people whose names literally couldn't be mentioned in my presence without me going apoplectic. Even if I didn't *say* anything, I seethed with rage or at least with resentment. The mere *thought* of someone on this list was enough for me to launch into one of my silent sermons in which I lectured them in great detail about everything they had done wrong. These mental gymnastics would often go on for hours. Not only that, I would literally plan where I would and wouldn't go based on an assessment of who *might* show up that I didn't want to deal with. (You remember that part about me being in *ministry*, right?)

God help my poor children. It's a wonder they're not both atheists. Or ex-churchgoers. (I owe *that* miracle to **The Special Blessings Prayer**, but more on that later.)

It took a nanosecond for my scribbled list to grow to forty names. Yours might be shorter. It might even be longer. The key is to make the list. So stop what you are doing right now. Don't read any further. Grab some paper or an electronic spreadsheet and make a list of every person who has hurt you *and it still hurts*. What's the test? The mention of their name causes a twinge of pain. Or maybe unleashes a flood-gate of emotions.

If the person hurt you and it still hurts—at all—put them on the list. Please don't move on to the next chapter until your list is ready. You cannot pray **The Special Blessings Prayer** without your list.

Your Assignment for This Chapter: Make your list of people who have hurt you. As you work through the book, you will be adding columns to this list so structure accordingly. [1]

---

1 If you would like to download a spreadsheet template to create your Special Blessings list, visit www.specialblessingsprayer.com/list

3. Determine What You Are Owed

I like David. A lot. One of my favorite things about David has always been that he prayed imprecatory prayers. Admit it: imprecatory is a seriously cool word. (I love words!) Have you ever heard it before? Imprecatory prayers *invoke evil upon* or *curse* one's enemies. Isn't that fabulous? We can pray special prayers that *invoke evil* and *curse* our enemies. And it's in the Bible! Yippee!

Here's a good one: "May their path be dark and slippery, with the angel of the LORD pursuing them" (Psalm 35:6). Of course, this is not a nice angel in a white dress; this is an avenging angel with a sword who looks really mean. Check out *The Bible* miniseries for some epic examples of these angels. Or how about: "O God, break the teeth in their mouths" (Psalm 58:6, ESV) That's a good one, too. I used to have terrible nightmares about my teeth breaking and falling out. It was terrifying! Awful. So yeah, this would definitely be a good imprecatory prayer to pray against some of those people on my list.

David wrote entire imprecatory prayer songs, asking God to bring judgment upon his enemies, including Psalms 7, 35, 55, 58, 59, 69, 109 and 139. David really didn't like it when people did him wrong. And frankly, it tended not to turn out real well for them, either.

Throughout the remainder of this book, we'll be looking in great detail at one example of someone who did David wrong. Just to give you some context, approximately sixteen years had passed since David was catapulted to national acclaim by his victory over Goliath. But at this point in his life, David's shining moment of glory probably felt like forever ago.

King Saul tried to kill him and drove him out of town in a fit of jealous rage. David was living out in the middle of nowhere—but not on a beautiful tropical island like the one I'm sitting on sipping Fiji Water. No, he was out in the barren Middle Eastern desert somewhere. And basically, he'd been running a mafia-style protection racket for local businessmen.

No. For real.

The idea is, David and his band of wild men (think motorcycle-gang members on camels) would hang out in the neighborhood and scare off anyone or anything that showed up looking even more dangerous than they are. That's what had come of the prophecy that he would be king someday. Kinda frustrating, right?

Maybe you've been there. A long time ago, someone prophesied greatness over you. Maybe it was a parent or a teacher, a prophet or a priest. But someone looked you in the eye and said, "God's gonna do great things in your life." And you believed it. For awhile. But then life happened and it reached a point where it seemed hopeless.

Or maybe you had great victories in the past but someone—a King Saul—became jealous and drove you out of town (or out of church or out of a job or whatever). Or maybe it wasn't a person; maybe it was the economy. I meet so many people who were successful at something in the past, but then they hit a crisis—lost a job, lost investments, lost a home—and their confidence had been shaken to the core. Nothing in life made sense anymore. Maybe that's you.

So here's David out in the desert; let's pick up the story in 1 Samuel 25:

> *Now Samuel died, and all Israel assembled and mourned for him; and they buried him at his home in Ramah. Then David moved down into the Desert of Paran. A certain man in Maon, who had property there at Carmel, was very wealthy. He had a thousand goats and three thousand sheep, which he was shearing in Carmel. His name was Nabal. (vs. 1-3)*

You didn't have a Mercedes back then, you just had a lot of sheep and goats. This is a seriously rich guy and wow, that's a *lot* of sheep. By any standard, three thousand sheep is not a sheep shortage. Remember that little detail as we continue with this story:

> *While David was in the desert, he heard that Nabal was shearing sheep. So he sent ten young men and said to them, "Go up to Nabal at Carmel and greet him in my name. Say to him, 'Long life to you! Good health to you and your household! Good health to all that is yours!*
>
> *"'Now I hear that it is sheep-shearing time. When your shepherds were with us, we did not mistreat them and the whole time they were at Carmel nothing of theirs was missing. Ask your own servants and they will tell you.*
>
> *"'Therefore be favorable toward my men, since we come at a festive time. Please give your servants and your son David whatever you can find for them.'" (vs. 4-8)*

Nabal's response was to turn him down flat.

Now we're getting to the heart of the matter and the point of this chapter. We're getting to what David was owed. David and his little gang had been protecting Nabal's stuff and, in return, they were expecting to get free meals. Stop by some Italian restaurants in South Philly, my friend; there are still certain people who get free meals in return for protection. It's probably best if I don't reveal much more about how or why I know this stuff, so let's move along.

So anyway, David's men went to Nabal and said, "*Hey, nothing bad happened to you because we've been watching out for you. And we're hungry. Can we get that free food now?*"

David, with the help of his men, had done all this work upfront without pay. With a kind of *gentleman's agreement* that when it came time to shear the sheep for food and wool, he would be compensated for all the work that he'd done.

If you understand the culture, he wasn't asking anything out of the ordinary. That's the way things worked back then: You take care of someone else and they take care of you. They didn't have all these commercials that you see on TV inviting you to file a civil suit at the drop of a hat. It was a gentlemen's agreement. David had done the right thing expecting—***assuming***—that because he'd held up his side of the bargain that, in turn, this wealthy man was also going to do the right thing.

Nabal was going to compensate him for all the work that he'd already provided. He was going to pay what David was owed.

Now how many of us have been there? Maybe even as a spouse, maybe as a parent, maybe as a member of the church or on the job. There's an unspoken agreement here:

- ✦ You do the right thing, you hold up your end of the bargain, and the other person or organization will do the same.
- ✦ You be a faithful spouse and in turn your spouse will be faithful to you.
- ✦ You be the best parent you know how to be and in turn your children will honor you.
- ✦ You work as hard as you can doing *whatever* and in turn you'll be compensated in some way.

We all operate every day based on these unwritten contracts that we have with the people around us. *We'll do the right thing by you and we trust that you're going to do the right thing by us.*

But how many of us know that's not always what happens? Sometimes we hold up our end of the bargain and then it comes time for us to get our recompense and we are treated with contempt.

Every person on your list is on your list for one very simple reason: **they owed you something,** whether love, respect, safety, support, encouragement, credit, common decency, a normal childhood, the truth, money, position, opportunity and the list goes on. What was it? What do you feel that person owed you?

David was owed sheep. What were you owed?

And you will recall, the guy who owed him sheep had three thousand of the little critters. So he had plenty to spare. It would have been the easiest thing in the world for him to help David out…but he chose not to. I'm wondering how many people on your list fall into that category? They *could* have helped you, maybe they even *should* have helped you…but simply chose not to.

It's not what they did; it's what they *didn't do* that hurts so much.

In the Lord's Prayer, we're instructed to pray, "Forgive us our debts, as we forgive our debtors." The first step in forgiving your debtor is determining exactly what debt you were owed. So go back to your list. And next to each name, I want you to write:

What did that person **owe** you? Do not move forward until you have completed this assignment.

Your Assignment for This Chapter: Indicate next to each name on the list exactly what that person owed you. Be as specific as possible.[2]

---

2 If you would like to download a spreadsheet template to create your Special Blessings list, visit www.specialblessingsprayer.com/list

4. Change One Variable, Change the Entire Equation

We interrupt our list-making activities to explore an equation:

$$O = E \times R$$

where O represents the Outcome or **"What your life ends up looking like."**

E represents the Experiences that set the wheels in motion that ultimately impact the Outcome. What makes life feel so hard is that very often the Experiences that seem to have the greatest impact on our lives are shaped not by us but by people around us. And that can be a terrifying, maddening, powerless feeling.

It's where we get the term "victim of circumstances." Ever feel like a victim of circumstances? Ever feel like your life looks the way it does not because of who you are or the choices you've made but because of people and circumstances you are completely incapable of changing? Ever feel like your life is spinning out of control or in a downward spiral but it's not your fault?

If so, I have some very good news for you today. **The R Factor.**

Even though it *seems* true, it's *not true* that your life is shaped primarily by your experiences—how you were raised, how you've been treated, bad stuff that's happened. Those things are *a* factor but they're definitely not the major factor. The major factor determining "what your life looks like" is the R Factor. Or how you choose to Respond.

Because when you change R, you change everything.

When you change R, you change the entire equation.

I want to go back in this 1 Samuel 25 passage to a few verses we skipped and introduce you to a woman who understood the R Factor. We've been talking about an unwritten agreement between David and a wealthy man named Nabal. We missed the part where the Bible tells us some important information about both the man and his wife.

> *His name was Nabal and his wife's name was Abigail. She was an intelligent and beautiful woman, but her husband was surly and mean in his dealings—he was a Calebite. (v. 3)*

We see through the example of Abigail that it's possible for you to be intelligent and beautiful and still have a lousy husband. But maybe it's even more important to know this: It's possible to have a surly, mean husband and still be absolutely terrific. Even though her husband was surly and mean and basically a terrible guy, that did not prevent Abigail from becoming the woman that God wanted her to be.

We need to get ahold of that because it is so easy for us to point to the people around us: our spouse, our children, our mother, our mother-in-law, our dad, our pastor, our next-door neighbor. And say, *"There's no way I can become the person I want to be, the person I know in my heart is my destiny, when I've got people like this in my life."*

If you think O = E, you're missing the most important part of life's equation.

Your life is not what your life experiences have made it; your life is what your experiences ***multiplied by*** your responses to those experiences have made it.

If Abigail's husband was surly and mean in general, I guarantee he was surly and mean to her in particular. But it didn't make her surly and mean. She didn't have to become like him just because she lived with him. Abigail was intelligent and beautiful. She didn't *let herself go*—like a lot of women do—to "punish" her husband. She took care of herself. And she didn't hold back her intelligence because it might be a threat to her husband. Instead, she allowed herself to become who God had created her to be. She didn't let this man drag her down. Or change the way she showed up in the world.

So enough with blaming our spouses for how we look and how we show up in the world. Speaking of spouses (or in this case, future spouse, but I'm getting way ahead of the story), let's get back to David.

Who was FREAKING OUT.

He was absolutely furious and threatened to kill every male member of Abigail's family because of what her husband had done. Wow, talk about crazy events unfolding that are completely out of your control! Her husband literally brought a death sentence down on her family. I don't know what you're up against right now, but is anyone threatening to kill you? I don't know what mistakes your loved ones have made, but have any of them put your life in jeopardy as a result? Could be.

How do you think you would respond if a disaster like this was looming over you?

Would you blame your husband? Would you blame David for over-reacting? Would you be immobilized by anger or fear? Would you climb under the covers in the fetal position, eating Oreos and pitching a pity party? Or would you rise to the occasion, carefully craft your response…and change the outcome entirely?

How do you respond in a crisis? Be honest.

So here's the crisis she's facing:

> *One of the servants told Abigail, Nabal's wife, "David sent messengers from the wilderness to give our master his greetings, but he hurled insults at them. Yet these men were very good to us. They did not mistreat us, and the whole time we were out in the fields near them nothing was missing. Night and day they were a wall around us the whole time we were herding our sheep near them. Now think it over and see what you can do, because disaster is hanging over our master and his whole household. He is such a wicked man that no one can talk to him." (vs. 14-17)*

Sometimes you're living with a person who is making bad decisions. And you feel like disaster is hanging—not just over that person but over the whole household—and you are swept up in it. These are the objective facts. And denying them won't help. It's not like Abigail had a few arguments with her husband and suddenly thinks he's terrible even though everyone else knows he's pretty terrific.

No. Here we see that the people *who work for him* all agree: he's a wicked man and no one can tell him anything. You can tell a lot about a person by what his or her co-workers think—and especially what support staff think (because we all tend to butter up the boss and higher-ups). So this story isn't about a marital spat. This is about a woman whose husband is a real problem.

But she doesn't let her problem husband become her project.

Do you live with someone who has become your "project"? You're going to fix that person or die trying? Abigail didn't make Nabal her project. She knew exactly who he was and learned to adapt herself accordingly. Notice, for example, she didn't try to go talk some sense into him because she already knew there was no sense in talking to him:

> *But she did not tell her husband Nabal. (v. 19)*

She gave her husband permission to be the person he wanted to be. He wanted to be mean and angry and selfish. Some people are so committed to staying the way they are that they are incapable of being anything you need them to be. So be it. They are the ones who will suffer for it.

I wonder what wonderful things you could accomplish with all that extra free time you'd have on your hands if you would quit wasting time trying to change people who have no intention of changing. Wouldn't it be fun to find out?

Now watch what Abigail did. Because as you'll soon see, her response dramatically changed the equation and the final outcome. Meanwhile, she prepared for the worst. Because David was marching toward Carmel. Now we all love David, that great psalmist of Israel, the man after God's own heart. But at this particular moment, we should pause to remember that he had already killed tens of thousands of people. Remember the song: Saul has killed his thousands and David tens of thousands? Those weren't just words to a catchy tune. Those were the facts.

When David heard the news that Nabal wasn't going to pay the debt he owed, he was ready to kill. Literal-ly.

> *David's men turned around and went back. When they arrived, they reported every word. David said to his men, "Each of you strap on your sword!" So they did, and David strapped his on as well. About four hundred men went up with David, while two hundred stayed with the supplies. (vs. 12-13)*

So now we have four hundred fierce warriors, led by a man who could single-handedly kill a thousand men and sleep like a baby the same night…and they are marching toward Abigail's house with swords drawn.

Disaster is literally hanging over her whole household and you'd better believe it because I'll tell you what: David and his army? ***They are fighting mad.*** They are marching toward Carmel to avenge a mistreatment. And when someone is marching towards Carmel, spitting mad, sword drawn, coming to avenge a perceived slight and to a collect a debt—it's going to get ugly.

Have you ever been in that place?

Someone has done something to you and *that's it*. You've had it! This time, you're putting an end to the madness. Enough of the abuse! Stop the insanity! You're going to pick up the phone and give them a piece of your mind. You're going to march into the pastor's office and tell him what's what. You're going to get all up in your co-workers' business and set them straight, once and for all. Or how about this one: you're going to write a scathing e-mail and hit send.

Don't you wish computers had an un-send button?

I don't even want to think about how much trouble I've gotten myself into just by pressing the send button when I was in "marching toward Carmel" mode.

Here's one of the most hilarious stories from my childhood—and I guess I can tell this now because the statute of limitations has run out on his original crime anyway. So here goes. My brother John was suspended from high school for smoking pot. But he swore to the highest heavens he hadn't been smoking pot. He even "swore on Coco's grave" which in our family was a vow stronger than marriage. If you "swore on Coco's grave" that settled it.

Well, my mother was spitting mad over the injustice! She was tired of her kids getting kicked around and falsely accused. Armed with the truth and the oath "sworn on Coco's grave," she strapped on her sword, hopped in her gold Cadillac Seville, drove to the school and marched into the principal's office.

By Job, her son was owed an apology. He was owed a clean record. This was an injustice! When would the outrageous slanders against our family end? The vice principal calmly looked at my brother and said, "John, I saw you with the joint in your hand." To which he replied with equal calm, "Yeah, but I wasn't smoking it. I was passing it."

Let's just say my mother marched out the door in a very different direction and it didn't turn out too well for my brother when my father got home.

How many times have we been marching toward Carmel, sword drawn, ready to demand what we thought we were owed? Because we've been mistreated. We've done all the right things! We are absolutely certain that we are 100 percent in the right, the other person is 100 percent in the wrong and there is no other choice but to seek justice. To exact revenge! To demand our pound of flesh!

In that moment of madness, you need to remember the R Factor. And because that's probably the last thing you're likely to think of in the midst of a massive adrenaline rush, maybe the best you can do is pray that God sends someone to remind you.

In that moment of madness, pray God will send you an Abigail. Someone with a good head on her shoulders who can calmly show you, "You're not seeing the bigger picture here. Right now, you think flipping out is the only possible response. But let me show you an alternative. Let me show you how this whole sorry mess can turn out completely differently if you choose a different response."

That's what she's about to do for David. And I hope and pray, it's what I'm about to do for you. So stay with me.

This story is not going to end with Abigail's family murdered and David left with yet more blood on his hands. She's going to show him the R Factor. I'll tell you more about that in a coming chapter. For now, I just want you to reread your list, the list of all the people who hurt you and what you thought they owed you. And I want you to consider this:

Is there any possible way you could have responded differently and had a very different outcome?

I'm not asking you to decide what that response should have been. Not yet. For now, just be open to the idea that even though you went through a horrible Experience with that person, the Outcome was never a foregone conclusion. A different Response from you—the R Factor—could have changed things quite dramatically. And in some cases, it's not too late for the R Factor to rescue you from a disastrous outcome in that relationship.

Please do not move on to the next chapter until you have looked at every person on your list and discovered at least one possible Response that might have resulted in a very different turn of events.

Now I have to give an incredibly important caveat here. If you were a child—I mean under the age of eighteen—then by definition you could *not* have responded any differently. So for now, do not worry about anyone on your list who hurt you before that age. We will deal with those cases later in the book. For now, I want you to go through your list and add another column to it: How you could have responded differently and had a very different outcome.

You are one step closer to experiencing **The Special Blessings Prayer**. I promise you, God's love, favor and power are about to be unleashed upon your life. But only if you fully participate in this process.

Your Assignment for This Chapter: For every person on your list, note at least one possible Response that might have resulted in a very different turn of events.

5. Rewrite the Story

We've looked at this story from the perspective of David, who has been cheated out of sheep by a guy who has three thousand of them. And we've looked at it from Abigail's perspective—a woman whose family is under threat of death because one family member made a terrible decision. But what about Nabal? What's his version of events?

My mom raised eight kids so if there was one lesson pounded into our precious little heads, it was this:

There are always two sides to every story.

Her mission was to listen to the various accounts and try to find the truth, which was usually somewhere in the middle. Few cases are black and white, cut and dried. So before we go any further, you're going to have to find a way to come to grips with this uncomfortable truth: The person who hurt you has his or her own version of events. And in that version of the story, *you* are the problem. You are the villain and the other person is the one who has been put upon, abused or mistreated. Trust me, I know how hard this is to accept. But it's true.

The Bible says in Proverbs 18:17, "The first person to speak in court always seems right until his opponent begins to question him." No matter how outrageous the crime, the criminal always justifies himself. *I had no choice. Actually, I'm the victim.* How often do you think someone walks into a courtroom and says, "I was completely to blame. I'm 100 percent at fault. You should throw the book at me"? No, they show up with their version of events and their bag of excuses and the list of reasons why they should not be held accountable for their own behavior.

The new standard defense seems to be this: "The mere fact that my client committed this hideous crime proves she's insane. No sane person would have done such a thing. Therefore, my client is innocent by reason of insanity." Actually, the insanity is a justice system that lets lawyers peddle this nonsense with a straight face.

One thing I greatly admire about Martha Stewart is how she handled her court case. Even though we all know that same sort of insider trading goes on all day, every day, when they brought the facts of the case to her attention and informed her what she had done was against the law, she said, "Fine, I'm guilty. I'll serve the time, pay the price and move on with my life."

And that's exactly what she did. It's almost enough to make me want to go to K-Mart and buy some of her stuff. Almost. But not quite.

A friend of mine (let's call him Bob) recently told me about an absolutely bizarre event that happened to him nearly twenty years ago. Bob's brother-in-law invited him to play golf with a couple other relatives. They hopped in the car and got on a Los Angeles freeway. Before long, Bob's brother-in-law was swept up into a road rage incident that had him driving nearly 120 miles per hour while Bob held on in the back seat in fear for his life. The guy followed the other driver when he took an exit ramp, forced him off the road, jumped out of the car and—with the help of the two other men—began beating the daylights out of the driver. Three against one.

Who knew a *golf outing* could turn that ugly?

Bob sat in the car in abject shock, not knowing what to do...but certainly unable to talk these three men out of their insane rage. Just then, a cop showed up and arrested the three men and threw them in jail. The other driver was severely injured and the case ended up in court.

You'll never guess who Bob's *sister* thinks is the villain in this story.

Yep: Bob. Bob's the bad guy because he refused to commit perjury in court. He says he didn't volunteer any additional information, but was required by law to honestly answer the questions he was asked under oath. His sister has never spoken to him again. If she were making her list right now, it would include:

Who	Debt Owed
My Brother	Lie in court

I know this story sounds ridiculous…but I can't help wondering how many of the people on your list would tell a *completely different version of events* than you are telling yourself right now. And in *their version,* you are the problem. You are the villain. You are the one who owed them.

In Nabal's version of events, David is the problem. But I'll let Nabal tell you about that in his own words:

> *When David's men arrived, they gave Nabal the message in David's name and then they waited. Nabal answered David's servants, "Who is this David? Who is this son of Jesse?" (vs. 9-10)*

My first reaction is: Look, dude, you know exactly who David is. He's already defeated Goliath. He's already well-known for fighting great battles on behalf of king and country. And surely Nabal already knows that David has been out there in the wilderness, knocking himself out to keep the sheep and shepherds safe. I don't think Nabal's being honest; I think he's playing a game.

But I'm saying that because I like David. I'm on his side. Nabal doesn't see it that way. He doesn't see David as a hero. He sees him as an outlaw. How do I know that's his perspective? He tells us:

> *"Many servants are breaking away from their masters these days." (v. 10)*

Because we've read the Book, we know this is a distorted view of events. But can we be certain Nabal knew? Doesn't seem like a guy who'd sit around reading the Bible even if the good parts about David had been written…and they hadn't been. We know, because we have the benefit of hindsight, that at every turn David had done the right thing and had been mistreated by King Saul. King Saul was trying to kill him out of sheer jealousy. It's not true that David was just a "servant breaking away from his master." He was the king's *son-in-law* who ran for his life from a crazy man.

But people twist things, don't they? And stories get told from person to person. You can be certain King Saul's people worked around the clock to discredit David. The smear campaign obviously worked. Note what Nabal says next:

> *"Why should I take my bread and water and the meat I've slaughtered for my shearers and give it to men coming from who knows where?" (v. 11)*

Who knows where? Where were the men coming from? From protecting his stuff. Working and being faithful and diligent. Operating in trust that because they were doing the right thing, that they would be treated fairly. That's not just David's version of events. It's the version collaborated by Nabal's own staff:

> *"The whole time we were out in the fields near them nothing was missing. Night and day they were a wall around us the whole time we were herding our sheep near them." (vs. 15-16)*

But Nabal doesn't see it that way. He thinks he's being taken for a ride. He is a rich man and one thing I know about rich people is that *everyone* around them feels *entitled* to a piece of the action.

Lottery winners are the best example. I'm not going to stop writing this book to go confirm the statistics, but I know they're insane. Something like 90 percent of them go bankrupt. Why? Some of it is blowing money on themselves, buying stupid stuff they don't need. But in many cases it's because they never learned how to deal with the never-ending parade of people who feel *entitled* to other people's money. That's why you'll notice that the first thing big lotto winners do these days is get a lawyer, collect the check, then go into hiding. Because you can be sure they are BOMBARDED with demands for money within hours of going public, no matter where they try to hide.

Professional athletes are another example. How does someone like Mike Tyson, who earned half a billion dollars as a prize fighter end up *bankrupt?* Because he was surrounded, 24/7, by an entourage of people who thought they were owed something. And I guess he felt he owed them something, too.

I don't want to read too much into this passage, but I've known some rich people. And I know they've had to learn that they simply cannot say *yes* to everyone who wants financial help from them. The irony, of course, is that each individual supplicant thinks, *"With all that money, surely they can help a sister out."* They never turn around to see the long line behind them—a long line of *other people* who also think, *"With all that money, surely they can help a brother out."* It must get exasperating after awhile. I'm sure it reaches the point where they think, "I'm so sick of trying to sort through all these sob stories when half of them are complete fabrications. You know what? That's it. The answer to the entire world is NO."

There was a brief season in my life when I was flush with a little extra cash. Not *nearly* as much as people thought because, as an author, I'm lucky to make a dollar per book sold. In some cases, I've earned as little as twenty cents. But I had a few books that did exceptionally well, I was on a bunch of radio and TV shows, my life looked pretty glamorous and I did indeed have more money than I'd ever had before. My primary love language is gifts and one of my spiritual gifts is giving.

You can picture the rest.

Boy, was I stupidly generous with the money. Or maybe just plain stupid. And boy, did it fly through my fingers faster than the speed of light. Here a loan, there a loan, everywhere a loan loan. Not one person *ever* paid me back. Not one. It reached the point where I said, "Let's not even call it a loan. Here, just take the money."

Every time I went out to breakfast, lunch or dinner with anyone, I felt obligated to pay for *everyone*. And I wondered why there were always so many people who wanted to sit at my table. Yes, indeed, I had my very own entourage of church people. I admit: it was kinda fun! And it wasn't just restaurants. Whenever I went anywhere with anyone, I felt obligated to pay for everything. Someone spotted a dress she liked? I bought it! Something cute for the house? It's yours! Sure, come on over to our house! Pizza and soda for the whole sports team! Snacks and meals all weekend, every weekend, for every teenager within fifty miles. We can always order more pizza! Hey, what's a couple hundred bucks per weekend flying out the door?

Uh oh.

Looks like I just answered my own question about how Mike Tyson went bankrupt. And why I don't have a retirement nest egg.

Maybe Nabal was tired of footing the bill for everyone's take-out sheep kabob orders. I don't know. But this much is sure: In Nabal's version of events, David is just another in a long string of shiftless people who think they can shake down the local rich guy. And he's having none of it.

Now I'm not defending Nabal. The Bible tells us the man was a fool and I'm not going to argue with God. I'm merely trying to make a point that every person on *your list* has his or her own version of events. And in that version of events, the other person is completely justified.

I have worked through **The Special Blessings Prayer** with hundreds of people, especially in my online classes like The 90-Day Renewal, Beyond Breakthrough and 30 Days in the Presence of God's Power. And I can tell you that most lists include at least one rich relative who the person feels *could have* and *should have* helped out financially and didn't. Or relatives who supposedly made off with more than their fair share of the inheritance. It's almost universal.

You can probably guess what I'm going to ask you to do next. I want you to go back to your list and add a column, "Their Version." If you want to experience the power of **The Special Blessings Prayer**, let me tell you a huge secret. And yes, I've done this for myself and it flat-out works. Pretend you are that person's Defense Attorney and argue as strenuously as you can for his or her innocence. Put together a winning case! Argue it!

This will sound crazy, but is so incredibly powerful: **Record** yourself passionately arguing their side of the story. And arguing like you mean it. Really imagine: What would *that person* say in their defense and how would they successfully portray *you* as the villain? Listen to it over and over again until you start to actually believe the other person might just have a valid point or two.

I can't even begin to tell you how healing this exercise can be for you. Try it. And the harder it is, the more you must force yourself to do it. The more convinced you are that the other person is 100 percent totally and completely in the wrong, and no sane person could possibly side with them, the more powerful this exercise has the potential to be.

Remember the caveat: This doesn't apply to anything that happened to you before the age of eighteen. Nor does it apply to literal criminal acts[3] committed against you, violence or abuse of any kind. We'll deal with forgiving the unforgivable later. For now, go through your list of ordinary offenses and take time to sincerely consider: What is their version of events?

You're one step closer to freedom because someone is waiting for you in the next chapter, ready to provide ***everything*** you truly need.

Your Assignment for This Chapter: Become the Defense Attorney for everyone on your list. Record your most passionate defense as an audio and listen to it over and over. Create a new column entitled: Their Version of Events.

---

[3] Do be careful not to twist every offense against you into a crime. I've seen people do that and it's counter-productive. For example, your sister got 70 percent of the inheritance and you think that's a crime. Or someone wrote a sub-prime mortgage for you or the insurance company did this, that or the other. I'm talking about rape, robbery, murder, and so on.

6. Would You Accept It from His Hands?

Let's get back to David. And what we was owed. What he thought he needed: sheep. And because Nabal, for whatever reason, is refusing to pay that debt and provide for that need, David is marching toward Carmel, sword drawn, ready to kill.

> *David had just said, "It's been useless—all my watching over this fellow's property, all that I've done for him, nothing of his was missing. He has paid me back evil for good. May God deal with David, be it ever so severely, if by morning I leave alive one male of all who belong to him!" (vs. 21-22)*

Can you relate? Ever been at that place? The place where you hear yourself muttering, *"After all that I've done for him, this is the thanks I get?"* Of course you have! We all have! Do you know what I call the Four Words of Doom?

After everything I've done

Yep, the Four Words of Doom. The four words that have foreshadowed every personal apocalypse in my life. Typically, after I've said those four words, I end up eating a half-gallon of Breyer's Mint Chocolate

Chip ice cream and watching *Out of Africa* or a Downton Abbey marathon.

After everything I've done.

I wonder how many people are on your list…because after everything you've done, where's the thanks?

I haven't yet adopted David's line "be it ever so severely," but I've got to say, I really do like it. And lately, I've been watching for a good opportunity to use it. Can't you just hear me? "After everything I've done for you kids, may God deal with me, be it ever so severely, if I don't eat an entire gallon of ice cream before bed tonight!"

After everything David did for this ungrateful spoiled-rotten rich guy, this is the thanks he gets? Well, he was fighting mad and somebody was going to pay. He was going to destroy not just Nabal but his entire household.

He saw no other course of action. But that doesn't mean there wasn't one. Abigail was about to show him that there *was* another way. Because while he was marching, God was working. And so was Abigail:

> *Abigail acted quickly. She took two hundred loaves of bread, two skins of wine, five dressed sheep, five seahs of roasted grain, a hundred*

> *cakes of raisins and two hundred cakes of pressed figs, and loaded them on donkeys. Then she told her servants, "Go on ahead; I'll follow you." But she did not tell her husband Nabal. (v. 18-19)*

Let's stop for a second. In his original request, David didn't specify exactly what he had in mind All he said was "whatever you can find" (v. 8).

He basically said, "I know you're shearing the sheep. Hint. Hint. Can we please have some?" In his terse reply, Nabal mentioned sheep, along with bread and water. Apparently, wine and cake weren't even on his radar screen. Never even occurred to him that David would *dare* to ask for more than sheep, bread and water. And that's probably a realistic assessment of what David might have been expecting.

Notice that Abigail was positioned to deliver an abundance of food to David. She prepared a literal feast. Whether it was more than he could have asked or imagined, I can't say for a fact, but it sure looks above and beyond to me.

Not just sheep, but bread, wine, grain, raisin and fig cakes.

I'm not going to touch the verse about not consulting her husband, because this isn't a marriage book. The Bible never condemns her for it and, in fact, she was richly rewarded for the series of choices she made without spousal consent. Is it ideal? Obviously not. But sometimes, in the real world, we have to deal with less than perfect circumstances and make the best of a bad situation. We already know he's surly and mean and doesn't listen to anyone anyway. So what would be the point?

She was in a crisis here. And when you're in a crisis and need to act fast, it's probably better not to bring a known troublemaker into the mix. And by the way, a crisis is not the right time to try to fix the most broken person you know. So forget the adage about "not letting a crisis go to waste." You can't afford to leverage *teachable moments,* make declarations of *I told you so* or rehearse a litany of all the *other problems* the person has created.

Just focus on your own response. That should be more than enough to keep you busy.

We're not told exactly how much time had transpired, we're only told "she lost no time." This woman must have had an extremely well-run household if she was able to throw together two hundred loaves of bread, five dressed sheep and enough wine and dessert to go with it in a hurry. It's not like she had a designer kitchen. So it's all the more impressive.

She got all of this food ready, then rode out to meet David.

Imagine the courage! Four hundred battle-hardened soldiers were coming to kill her family and rather than fleeing to the hills or looking for a place to hide, she rode out to meet them. It's like a scene from *The Lord of the Rings* except this actually happened and Gandalf was nowhere to be found. No army of elves coming at the crack of dawn. She was completely on her own. A woman alone. Riding on a donkey.

If you think I'm exaggerating the danger, let's pick up the story:

> *As she came riding her donkey into a mountain ravine, there were David and his men descending toward her, and she met them. (v. 20)*

Ever been *descended upon?* Ever feel like *you're suddenly being attacked?* It's an unsettling experience. These men are ready for battle, ready for war. And even though Abigail was an innocent bystander, she was the one in the crosshairs. Everyone she loved was at risk of becoming collateral damage in a conflict she had nothing to do with starting.

It doesn't specify what they are riding, but I will guarantee you one thing: they weren't riding donkeys. No one in a hurry rides a donkey. No one riding into battle rides a donkey. In Old Testament times, arriving on a donkey meant you came in peace. In the same way, a horse was a symbol of war. When you got on your horse, you were going to battle. That's why it's so significant that when Jesus entered Jerusalem on Palm Sunday, he wasn't riding a horse. He didn't come as a conquering King ready for political battle. He rode into Jerusalem—Jeru-shalom, the city of peace—riding a donkey, the symbol of peace.

If you picture David and his men astride decorated Arabian war horses, I don't think the image would be far off. But Abigail didn't meet them on their terms. She didn't conclude, *"Well, if it's a fight they want, it's a fight they'll get."* Quite the opposite. She defused the situation. Just because someone picks a fight with you, doesn't mean you have to join the battle. You can choose how you respond.

Every move Abigail made in this passage communicates, *"I'm not coming out to fight with you, David. If I wanted to fight with you, I would've hopped on a horse. And I would have brought all the people who are on* my side *with me."*

Abigail came to David riding a donkey, seeking to make peace. And she's got bread and wine and sheep with her. Does she remind you of anybody else?

- ✦ Jesus himself is the sheep; he's the Lamb of God sacrificed for our benefit.
- ✦ He comes to us offering the bread and the wine—the bread of his body and the wine of his blood.

- ✦ He comes riding a donkey on Palm Sunday—riding toward his sacrificial destiny at Calvary.

- ✦ He comes to make peace, putting himself in between two warring parties: the Judge of Heaven who requires payment for sin...and lost sinners incapable of ever repaying the debt we owe.

Could it be any more obvious that Abigail is an Old Testament picture of Jesus?

She came riding on her donkey, offering payment to the future king for the debt her husband owes. A debt he is incapable of paying, not because of what he does or does not have (wealth), but because of *who he is* (a foolish sinner).

But it is much more than that. She came offering not just the debt owed but *everything David needed*. She came with *more* than he would have dared to ask for. She even sweetened the gift with delicious desserts. The Bible tell us that God gives immeasurably more than all we could ask or imagine and that every good and perfect gift is from above. And that's exactly what we see here.

Maybe when you think about the people who've hurt you—the people on your list—you're fighting mad, too. You feel like this person or that person has cheated you or deprived you of your legitimate needs.

Jesus comes to you now, just like Abigail came to David, and he says,

> My child, I am both willing and able to give you everything you need. I understand why you're upset. You're upset because you genuinely needed __________ (fill in the blank). That's why you're fighting mad. That's why you've got your sword drawn. That's why you're ready to kill someone. You feel like you needed something and it's not been provided to you.
>
> But child, you are mistaken if you think the only way to make this pain go away is if that person repays the debt. I'm standing here right now offering you everything you really need. Why don't you put your sword away? Put your words away. Put the hurt away.
>
> It will help if you try to understand this: The person who mistreated you is entirely incapable of holding up his or her end of the bargain, doing the right thing and meeting your legitimate needs. It's not going to happen.
>
> So you can just keep right on marching and go try to get your revenge. But you're not going to get what you need. If you want what

> you need, lay down your weapons. I'm standing right here, right now and I will give you —free of charge—immeasurably more than you've ever asked or imagined.

I've been a Christian for thirty years and did not get the story of Abigail until God knocked me over the head with it a few years back.

Who are you fighting mad at? Is it possible that God is more than capable of giving you not only what that person owed you *but even more than you would have dared to ask for?*

We're going to come back and go into greater detail about what transpired between Abigail and David, but for our purposes right now, here's the punchline:

> *Then David accepted from her hand what she had brought him. (v. 35)*

Right now, you may be very attached to the idea that *the person who owes you* is the only acceptable person to repay you. But is that really true?

Pause. Ponder. Repeat.

Right now, you may be very attached to the idea that *the person who owes you* is the only acceptable person to repay you. But is that really true? What difference does it make *who pays* as long as you get everything you need…and more?

Let me come at this from another direction. If it matters to you *who* repays the debt, than it's not really about the debt anymore. It's not about what you were owed, what you were cheated out of and what you legitimately need; it's about punishment and revenge.

So just be honest about that.

If it matters to you *who repays the debt,* then it's no longer about the other person. It's about you. And you are now the one clearly in the wrong. Because you are in direct defiance of God who says, "It is mine to avenge, I will repay."

If the only issue at stake is your legitimate needs, then it should not matter *at all* how God choses to provide. God is asking you the same question Abigail asked David, *"Will you accept from my hand what I want to give you? Stop looking to that person who you think owes you something. Receive it from me instead."*

So your assignment for this chapter should be clear by now. Add another column to your list. In what way might God himself *repay that debt?*

✦ If you were cheated out of love, know that God *is* love.

- If you were robbed financially, God owns the cattle on a thousand hills. He can meet all your needs according to his riches in glory.

- If you were dishonored and disrespected, God offers you a place of honor and respect as a child of the King, as part of a royal priesthood, a holy nation, his ambassador.

- If you were passed over for a promotion you deserved, the Bible clearly reveals that promotion is from the Lord. He elevates one and casts down another. If he can direct the heart of kings, he can direct someone in authority over you to promote you.

- Did someone drive you out of your house? God can easily find you a better one. Or does that sound too hard for the Ruler of the universe?

- Did you miss out on being raised in a safe, loving home? God can give you the wisdom and grace to create one of your own. And you'll have the advantage of not taking it for granted.

These are just a few examples. Ask God to show you, specific to your situation, how he is more than capable of repaying any and every debt you are owed.

In some cases, you may suddenly realize: ***He already has.***

He already has, hasn't he? If you can find the YES in your heart, the healing and power of **The Special Blessings Prayer** will already begin to be unleashed in you.

Your Assignment for This Chapter: Add a column "How might God repay the debt?"

7. Place The Blame In the Right Place

When life hurts, when things don't turn out the way we hope or expect, we want someone to blame. David's world had completely fallen apart. He'd been waging an internal struggle to resist lashing out at his father-in-law, King Saul, the one man who actually deserved the blame. But now along comes Nabal who, in the case of the undelivered sheep, becomes a convenient scapegoat for everything that was wrong in his life.

Think about it. If David were still living in the king's palace, he wouldn't need a handful of sheep from Nabal. A lot of times we're mad at someone for not helping us out when that person had *nothing whatsoever to do* with the long series of events that brought us to the place of *needing* help. In other words, *we're mad at the wrong person*. David refused to take revenge on his father-in-law who repeatedly tried to kill him, gave his wife away to another man, drove him into exile and was busy spreading horrible rumors about him. And we applaud David for declaring, "I will touch not the Lord's anointed." But now he was ready to kill Nabal's entire family over some sheep.

Why do we do that? I don't know. But we do. We pick some random person to fixate on and lay every drop of blame for everything that's wrong in our lives squarely on their shoulders. Typically, we pick a family member. How many of us are still blaming our mom or dad or someone who hurt us as a five–year-old for *everything* that's wrong in our lives? I'm not trying to minimize the pain. I'm saying *no single event* and *no one person* is capable of defining your entire life without your consent.

David wanted to blame someone, *anyone*, for the mess he was in. So suddenly, it was all Nabal's fault. If it weren't for Nabal withholding those sheep, life would have been just fine and dandy. But without those sheep, the world was a terrible place; therefore, Nabal had to die. In this case, it's the *sheep* that broke the camel's back rather than the straw.

How many times have you been there? You go through crisis after crisis, loss after loss, and you're holding up pretty well. In fact, people are congratulating you about "how well you're doing under the circumstances." Then some customer service rep from the cable company gets on your last nerve and you blow a gasket. That person becomes the flash point for all of your pent up frustration and you *unleash*.

Or am I the only one?

Any objective person watching David in this situation can plainly see he is blowing this situation all out of proportion. Abigail sees that. That's why she doesn't state the obvious: *CHILL OUT. You are majorly overreacting, you psychopath!*

Instead, she looked past David's overreaction to see what was really going on. That's why she said, in essence, *"David, you obviously need someone to blame. Go ahead and blame me. I've got broad shoulders."*

> *When Abigail saw David, she quickly got off her donkey, bowed down before David with her face to the ground. She fell at his feet and said: "My lord, let the blame be on me alone." (vs. 23-24)*

Here again, we see Abigail as a type of Christ. She doesn't tell David he's wrong to feel hurt. She doesn't tell him he's a terrible, no-good guy. She simply gives David a safe place to vent his frustration. That's exactly what Jesus does for us. He comes riding to our emotional rescue and offers us a safe place to pour out all the hurt. He comes to us when we are fighting mad, when we've been wronged. When we've done all the right things and we've been mistreated. And we're marching to Carmel with swords drawn, seeking revenge.

That's when Jesus arrives on the scene to say, "Let the blame be on me alone. If you're looking for someone to blame, blame me. I've got broad shoulders. Shoulders that have already carried the weight of all the world's sin."

It's time to get the revelation:

Jesus did not just die to pay the price for every sin you've committed. He also died to pay the price for every sin committed against you.

We all understand the first part: that Jesus paid for our sins. But I'm not so sure we understand the full power of Calvary until we understand the second part. If we can wrap our hearts around this truth, we can walk in a degree of emotional wholeness that is entirely unavailable apart from the cross of Christ.

Because life hurts all of us. And if we have nowhere to take that pain, we will lash out at the people around us. Or we will internalize the hurt, allowing it to seep into our soul where it will do untold damage. But what if we took *every* sin to the cross? Not just our *own* sin—*every* sin. What if the moment someone sinned against us, we ran to the foot of the cross, looked into the face of the Prince of Peace and took him up on the offer: "*Let the blame be on me alone.*"

If Jesus already *paid in full* then there's no need to exact payment. There's no need to demand further compensation. There's no need for that person to be punished. It's all taken care of at the cross.

The story of David and Abigail is not just the story of Nabal's sin, although it is that. It's also the story of David's temptation to *respond to that sin* by sinning. And that's the story of all of our lives, isn't it? What trips most of us up isn't our own sin, but our sinful response to the sin of others. What Abigail provided for David was a way of escape when he faced the nearly overwhelming temptation to sin against a sinner. In doing so, she points us to Christ who gives us a way to escape that same temptation.

We have the power to choose to forgive because of the power of the cross.

Can you imagine how your life would change if you lived this way? What if you, like David, turned around and marched in the opposite direction? Rather than continue the march toward Carmel to demand repayment...what if you marched to Calvary instead and said, "*There's nothing this person needs to give me that Jesus didn't already die that I might freely receive*"?

What's the alternative? David tells us:

> *David said to Abigail, "Praise be to the LORD, the God of Israel, who has sent you today to*

> *meet me. May you be blessed for your good judgment and for keeping me from bloodshed this day and from avenging myself with my own hands. Otherwise, as surely as the* L*ORD, the God of Israel, lives, who has kept me from harming you, if you had not come quickly to meet me, not one male belonging to Nabal would have been left alive by daybreak." (vs. 32-34)*

If you refuse to march to Calvary and keep marching toward revenge, you might just destroy an entire household. How many families are torn apart by divorce each year? Not just because Mom and Dad go their separate ways, which is agonizing enough, but because they compound the pain by dragging each other into court and tearing each other down in front of the children. How many families are torn apart fighting over an inheritance? How many business and professional relationships are destroyed by lawsuits? How many church families split each year, as factions form and accusations are hurled back and forth?

All of this madness is exactly the opposite of what Scripture clearly commands: "Make every effort to live in peace with everyone and to be holy; without holiness no one will see the Lord. See to it that no one falls short of the grace of God and that no bitter root grows up to cause trouble and defile many" (Hebrews 12:14-15).

Why are we commanded to make every effort to live in peace? Because otherwise, a bitter root will defile many. And in many cases, not just defile, but destroy.

Some of you reading these words right now need to take heed: You could destroy an entire household if you keep marching in the direction you're heading. I implore you to make an about-face. Turn toward Calvary. Look full in his wonderful face and the things of this world will grow strangely dim in the light of his glory and *grace*.

Your Assignment for This Chapter: Go through your list, one by one, take each sin to the cross to accept the offer Jesus has made, "Let the blame be on me alone." Make up your mind that you are no longer going to respond to sin by sinning, because that is never the answer.

8. Look Past Your Pain

There are so many remarkable things about Abigail and how she handled this situation, but perhaps one of the most impressive is her ability to look beyond her own pain to see David's. She saw him not as her enemy, not as a man issuing death threats against her family, but as a desperate man.

And she fully understood why he was doing what he did, even though he was behaving irrationally. If only we would take just a moment to *put ourselves in that other person's place,* we might see the situation very differently. Every person who has ever hurt you, hurt you out of his or her own brokenness. Here's one of the truest truths in the world: hurt people hurt people.

I cried for David this morning. I cried for the man he momentarily became in this story. And for the tens of thousands of people in the world today who find themselves in a similar place of pain, loss and desperation.

Think of it. Once upon a time, David was a young man filled with promise. Plucked out of the shepherd's field and hand-picked by the mighty prophet Samuel, anointed the future king of Israel. His family didn't seem to put much stock in the prophecy because afterwards they sent him back out to the fields to watch over the flock in obscurity.

But I am certain David clung to that word and the dream it represented as he faithfully worked day and night protecting—of all things—sheep. Ironic, right? This whole conflict is about his desperation to get his hands on something he once had *more than enough of*.

We don't know how large his father's flock was, but it was apparently enough to be a fulltime job for David. We know he took the job seriously, because when he arrived in the Valley of Elah to deliver cheese and bread to his brothers on the frontline, he said—before fighting Goliath—that he had experience fighting both a lion and a bear.

I don't know about you, but if my family had so little respect for me that when the biggest big shot in the country came to dinner (in this case, the prophet Samuel), I wasn't even invited. And if my family believed so little in me that even after that prophet said I would someday do great things, they sent me right back to the fields without a drop of fanfare. If that's how I was treated, when a lion showed up to kill the family sheep, I wouldn't do battle with it. How would anyone know anyway? It's not like they had surveillance cameras.

My attitude would probably have been, "What do I care about their lousy sheep? They don't believe in me, why should I risk my life to protect their stuff?

Go ahead, lion, eat your heart out. Would you like some mint sauce with that?"

Not David. He had a track record of doing the right thing even when people didn't treat him right. He had a track record of doing the right thing even when no one was watching. He knew God was always watching. When he wrote in the twenty-third Psalm, "The Lord is my Shepherd," part of what he revealed is his understanding that although he was *a* shepherd, he answered to *the* Shepherd for every move he made.

I think it's one of the things God probably loved most about David. The Bible tells us the eyes of the Lord range throughout all the earth, looking for those whose hearts are fully committed to him. God is always watching us—not because he's looking for someone to punish, but because he's looking for someone to promote. Someone who can be trusted with a position of responsibility because he or she has been faithful in obscurity and has operated with integrity even when no one but God was watching.

We know defeating the lion wasn't a one-off thing, because he mentions killing a bear. People sometimes portray the battle between David and Goliath as a miracle. Or a fluke. But I think it was skill. And as we know, repetition is the mother of skill. David spent a lot of years practicing the skill of killing things with a sling shot. And that's the very skill God used to catapult him into national prominence.

And by the way, I don't think David selected five stones in case he missed with the first four. The Bible tells us Goliath had four brothers. I think he planned to take the whole family down. Notice he hadn't really changed his approach. He wasn't planning just to take down Nabal, he had enough ammunition to take the whole family down.

But one thing he didn't have anymore: sheep. He literally didn't have a single sheep of his own and had been reduced to watching over a stranger's sheep. Speaking of reduced. Don't forget that David's victory over Goliath led to many more victories, eventually resulting in his winning the hand of the king's daughter in marriage.

He lived at the king's court, as the king's son-in-law, a potential heir to the throne. Those days as a national icon, living in the lap of luxury, must have felt like a million years ago. And I wonder what that felt like? I wonder how humiliating it was for the former son-in-law of the king to be put in this position of living in caves and groveling for a few sheep?

A lot of people lost it all during the economic meltdown of 2008. People who once had high hopes and great expectations are now at a place of sheer desperation. People who once had a career, a home, a retirement account no longer have any of those things. They'd give anything to get back a fraction of what they once had and took for granted. Maybe that's where you're at right now. Or maybe that's how the people on your list feel. In the best of times, they never would have done such a thing to you or anyone else. But lately, many of us have had a taste of the worst of times, haven't we?

We are living in desperate times in America and many parts of the world. And in desperate times, even good people are tempted to do desperate things. That's where David was at in this scene. Think of it: He was ready to kill for a handful of sheep. He was the one who later said of Saul, "Oh how the mighty have fallen," but at this moment, the words are equally true of him.

I don't think Nabal was the only one he was frustrated with. I think he was frustrated with his life. I think the insults Nabal hurled at David hit their mark as accurately as the stone David once hurled at Goliath. His pride was at stake, not just his stomach. Notice how Nabal attacked David's *identity:*

> *"Who is this David? Who is this son of Jesse?" (v. 10)*

The questions hurt because David was probably asking those same questions. He may have begun to doubt himself and wonder about his future. We know how this story ends, but David didn't. We know he eventually ruled and reigned over one of the greatest earthly kingdoms in history. We know he eventually accumulated so much worldly wealth that he left an inheritance that his son Solomon was able to leverage to become the only documented trillionaire in human history. We know his descendent Jesus still sits on the throne David established and will continue that kingly dynasty throughout all eternity.

David didn't know he had a bright future. All he knew right then is the pain of this public humiliation and the frustration of the six hundred hungry men surrounding him. Abigail saw what he'd been reduced to…and had compassion on him. She spoke directly to the moment his world fell apart: the day King Saul turned against him and drove him into exile. The day he went from hero to zero in an instant:

> *"Even though someone is pursuing you to take your life." (v. 29)*

Abigail set aside her own pain long enough to see his. Could we do the same? I have long said the cure for anger is compassion. If you can find a way to see the person who hurt you not as a villain but as a hurting human soul, you'll be amazed how quickly wrath dissipates. I have experienced many times the beautiful truth that "mercy triumphs over justice."

One of the hardest people for me to deal with on my list was a man who sexually abused me throughout my childhood, beginning no later than the age of two. (I have specific memories at that age but there's compelling evidence that it started even younger.) Oddly enough, I had a harder time forgiving his wife, who would sleep on the couch so as not to disturb him while he molested countless children.

How could she do that? He was a monster. He was an evil pedophile. *What was her excuse? Why didn't she intervene? Why didn't she protect me?* I've been told this is common among victims—we blame the safer person, not the most frightening one. So I placed even *more blame* on the wife.

Then one day as I was praying **The Special Blessings Prayer**, the Lord asked me, "How would you like to be married to that terrifying, evil man?"

I was undone.

Suddenly, I was flooded with compassion for her. She was afraid of him and felt powerless to stop him. This was in a day when working-class women had very few options. Catholics certainly didn't get divorced and even if she did, how on earth would she provide for herself? She felt trapped. This doesn't make her inaction right; it doesn't justify it. But it helped me find a place inside of me, a place of compassion, that saw her pain and began to heal mine.

Forgiving my molester is a journey I'm still on; the healing has happened in stages and there's probably more that needs to happen. But what's helped me most, ironically, is traveling into the heart of darkness around the world, looking evil in the eye in places like war-torn communities in Africa or the sex-slave district of Bangkok. I have seen for myself how the devil treats his own. When you dance with the devil, he exacts a horrifying price. I'm sure the same demons who tormented me *through* that man inflicted even more torment *upon him*. What a tortured soul he must have been! In my strongest moments, I truly feel sorry for him.

Your Assignment for This Chapter: Can you find a way to look past your pain just long enough to see the other person's pain? Go through your list, one by one, and note the pain that may have been driving that person. And in many cases, the pain that still does.

9. What If That Person Really IS a Villain?

The likelihood that God sees anyone on your list as nothing more than a one-dimensional villain is fairly remote. But then again, it's not impossible. The Bible tells us God hated Esau. That he is angry with the wicked every day. Hey, this is a tough one: that he literally *fashioned* Pharaoh as an object of his wrath.

In this story, God clearly agreed with the general consensus that Nabal was a villain and punished him accordingly:

> *When Abigail went to Nabal, he was in the house holding a banquet like that of a king. He was in high spirits and very drunk. So she told him nothing at all until daybreak. Then in the morning, when Nabal was sober, his wife told him all these things, and his heart failed him and he became like a stone. About ten days later, the LORD struck Nabal and he died. (vs. 36-38)*

When I first read this story, I actually found it a bit shocking the way Abigail talked about her husband:

> *Please pay no attention, my lord, to that wicked man Nabal. He is just like his name—his name means Fool, and folly goes with him. (v. 25)*

Isn't this book about blessing people who've hurt us? Why doesn't Abigail have to bless Nabal? To bless means to ***speak well*** and even to ***think well*** of another person. She's certainly not speaking well or thinking well of her husband. If she's such a great biblical example, why isn't she praying **The Special Blessings Prayer** and walking through this whole process in relationship to her own husband?

I've been wrestling with that question for a few months and have come to the conclusion that circumstantial evidence supports the conclusion that she handled this relationship about as well as could be expected. More about that in a second. We know she said some pretty terrible things about him in the middle of a crisis. Whether it was her *habit* to talk about him like that, we simply do not know. I find that highly unlikely, based on everything else we observe about her character, but I can't argue that case from the text. We know that within twenty-four hours of this blow-up, her husband was in a catatonic state. And ten days after that, he was dead. What she did, how she prayed, the words she spoke sitting at his bedside—we simply have no way of knowing. My strong conviction is that God gave her enough time to make peace with him, so she could move on with a clear conscience. But I don't know that for a fact.

And speaking of what we don't know. We have no idea what happened prior to 1 Samuel 25. We don't know how horribly he treated her, although we do know he was mean and he may well have been an alcoholic. And few things on this earth are harder to endure than a ***mean drunk***. I'd rather not say much more about how I know so much about that. One little tidbit that supports the *mean drunk theory* is that she waited until he sobered up in the morning to try to talk with him. We have no idea what this man had put her through or how hard she had tried to make this marriage work.

There's a lot we don't know...but then again, there's a lot we do:

- ✦ We know she was beautiful—that she didn't let herself go.
- ✦ She ran her household extremely well—well enough to throw together a massive feast on a moment's notice.
- ✦ Her staff trusted her implicitly to make good decisions in a crisis.
- ✦ Her staff knew she was a safe person—the kind they could be completely honest with.

✦ Finally, we know God believed she deserved to become a queen.

I think when we add all of that up, we're safe to conclude that Abigail held herself with great dignity in a very difficult marriage. Do I think it would have been better if Abigail refrained from publicly insulting her husband? Frankly, I do. Do I think she could have presented her case to David with equal eloquence without throwing her husband under the bus in such dramatic fashion? Again, I do.

But God didn't ask my opinion. He does nothing but honor and elevate Abigail, so I agree with him. God looks at the totality of our character, not just stupid stuff we say in the middle of a crisis. Clearly she was afraid and was trying to distance herself from his actions:

> *"And as for me, your servant, I did not see the men my lord sent." (v. 25)*

They say hard cases make bad law. Nabal is certainly a hard case. Hard enough that God personally intervened and *took him out*. I looked for a way to gloss over this part of the passage, but that would have been disingenuous. We have to deal with the Scripture as it is. And we cannot escape the implication that it *is* possible that you might just have a genuine villain somewhere on that list. I'm reluctant to send you on a villain hunt, because I simply don't think it's helpful. Nevertheless, some factors to consider:

- ✦ Notice his or her behavioral tendency. Nabal had a long-standing history of being surly and mean. It's also pretty obvious he had a track record for getting falling-down drunk. Is what you suffered at the hands of this person part of a *pattern*? Or is it all the more painful and shocking because this is not like that person *at all?*

- ✦ Notice how other people view him or her. Everyone around Nabal said the exact same thing about him and it wasn't anything good. If everyone around someone on your list agrees he or she is terrible and you can't find a single person to say a kind word, you might have a genuine villain on your hands. But if everyone else thinks that person is terrific, you might want to factor that into the equation. You can fool some of the people some of the time but you can't fool all of the people all of the time. Surely, if you are dealing with a truly evil person, others have figured that out.

- ✦ There are exceptions. Recently, it's been all over the news that one of the most respected and seemingly trustworthy entertainers of the twentieth century was a serial rapist and a certifiable sociopath. So it could be your villain is *so evil* he's got the whole world fooled. But he certainly doesn't have

God fooled and you can be sure his sin will eventually find him out.

My strong admonition is to resist the temptation to try to make these sorts of judgments for yourself. In the last chapter, I shared openly about my struggle to forgive a child molester who inflicted great damage on my soul. Is he an example of an entirely villainous villain? Based on evidence I've heard from other victims and the large number of destroyed lives he left in his wake, it's quite possible. But even in that case, I've wrestled hard to leave that judgment where it belongs—in the hands of the Only Wise Judge, the one who has told us:

> *Do not take revenge, my dear friends, but leave room for God's wrath, for it is written: "It is mine to avenge; I will repay," says the Lord. (Romans 12:19)*

If God says he will repay, he will repay. Nabal is proof of that.

Your Assignment for This Chapter: If there is someone on your list who appears to be a genuine villain, rest in the knowledge that *God* will ultimately deal with that person.

10. Find Out What God Says about That Person

Having dealt with the villains, let's now turn our attention to the far more likely scenario that, for the most part, you are dealing with regular people who hurt you in some way. It might even be the case that some of the people on your list are profoundly loved by God and considered by him to be among his choicest servants. But at the time you encountered that person, he or she was going through a tough situation that temporarily brought out the worst.

Such was the case for David. David completely blew it in terms of his response to a fairly minor offense. If all we knew about David is that he freaked out over some sheep, we wouldn't like him at all. But there was more to David. Much more. And when we read the whole Bible and look at his whole life in balance, despite his many flaws, we just can't help seeing why God loved him so much. Even in this short passage about David at his worst, we see glimpses of David at his best:

1. He was trusting. He worked hard for Nabal with no assurance of repayment (v. 7).

2. He was protective (v. 16).

3. He bravely fought the Lord's battles (v. 28).

4. He was teachable. When Abigail helped him realize he was on the wrong path, he didn't hesitate to course correct (v. 35).

5. He left justice in God's hands (v. 39).

When we look at the *totality* of David's life, we see a complex multifaceted person who sincerely loved God, made a lot of mistakes, but always tried to do the best he could with the strength he had on any given day. In short, we see ourselves.

Isn't that who we all are? Human beings who have good days and bad days. Capable of amazing feats of faith one minute, unequal to a trip to the grocery store the next. Human beings in need of the grace of God…and heaping doses of grace from the people around us, too.

I've been a public figure in the Christian community since I was barely thirty years old, when I was catapulted onto the best-seller list and a nationwide speaking platform. I was still emotionally fragile from things that had happened to me in my childhood and drowning in the backwash of mistakes I'd made in my late teens. Nothing in my past had prepared me for the pressures of ministry. I had zero logistical support and no spiritual support system to speak of.

There I was, traipsing around the country, completely clueless about how to wrestle "against the rulers, against the authorities, against the powers of this dark world and against the spiritual forces of evil" coming against me (Ephesians 6:12).

As I result, I lost most of those wrestling matches and ended up face down on the mat, exhausted, defeated and filled with pain. I am absolutely certain that during that season of my life I had countless encounters with people who walked away thinking I was a terrible, no-good person. Actually, I was just a hurting person doing the best I could on any given day.

Probably a lot like you. And every person on your list.

I wonder. If you could find a way to look at the *totality* of each life represented on your list—not just a snapshot of how that person treated you in a specific situation which may very well represent that person at his or her very worst. I wonder if that might not give you a more accurate perspective.

Maybe you would see for yourself what God sees in that person. Because God sees beautiful things in every life he tenderly fashioned in the womb. God loves people. And he wants us to love them, too. He even tells us to *love* our enemies. Jesus said the most important commandments are to love God and love people:

> *"'Love the Lord your God with all your heart and with all your soul and with all your mind and with all your strength.' The second is this: 'Love your neighbor as yourself.' There is no commandment greater than these.'" (Mark 12:30-31)*

The Apostle Paul said:

> *The entire law is fulfilled in keeping this one command: "Love your neighbor as yourself." (Galatians 5:14)*

The disciple Jesus loved put it this way:

> *Everyone who loves has been born of God and knows God. Whoever does not love does not know God, because God is love. (1 John 4:7-8)*

God loves people. Including the people on your list. Love is God's priority. But since "love" can sometimes be an ephemeral thing, let's make it super-practical and focus on one specific way you can demonstrate love to the people on your list. Now don't panic. I'm not going to suggest inviting the entire list over for Christmas dinner. You don't have to buy each one a present or name your child after one of them.

I'm not talking about anything crazy or difficult. In fact, this idea is so simple to implement, you can do it even if you never speak to that person ever again as long as you live.

Are you ready? Here goes:

Stop talking about what they did to you.

Among the many things we know about love, we know that "love covers over a multitude of sins" (1 Peter 4:8). Proverbs 17:9 says, "Whoever would foster love covers over an offense, but whoever repeats the matter separates close friends."

The great thing about loving your list members in this way is that it's also an incredibly loving thing to do for yourself and everyone around you. The people who, by now, are probably sick and tired of hearing about this stuff. Your world will be exponentially better when you stop poisoning the atmosphere around you with negativity.

Can we take the pledge together today? *No* to rehashing. *No* to raking them over the coals. *No* to drawing attention to all their faults and follies. *No* to making sure everyone knows *what that person is REALLY like* and *what they did to you.* As of today, no more talking. As of today, start listening to hear what God has to say. And be open to the possibility that God just might want to tell you how wonderful he thinks some of the people on your list are and how much he loves them.

The beautiful thing about love is that it's an emotion. And emotions are contagious. The more you listen to God's heart for your list, the more you will find his love shed abroad in your heart. Then maybe, some miraculous day, you'll discover you love those people with a ***supernatural love*** that could only have come from God.

I can't help thinking that's what God did for Abigail. Clearly her words—like "the lives of your enemies he will hurl away as from the pocket of a sling"—were divinely inspired. When she spoke to David, she was speaking the very heart of God for him. I picture Abigail, slowly riding her donkey toward David, as God's perfect love cast out all her fears. As he gave her his blessed assurance, "*You are safe with my servant, David. I know him by name. He is mine. I would give men in exchange for his life. I chose him before the foundations of the world to fight my battles for me. He is precious in my sight and, daughter, know this: Not one promise I have made to that man will be left unfulfilled.*"

I see a smile coming across her lips and tears streaming down her face. I can see it happening to her because it just happened to me…as God poured out his heart for David through my keyboard.

Oh what joy could be yours! What freedom from fear and pain if you would invite God to share his heart with you! His heart for each and every name on your list. You may believe the very worst about those people—that they are lost causes. But God believes the best: He sees a hope and a future for every one of them. Because God is love and love believes the best (1 Cor. 13:7).

Listening for God's heart is going to be absolutely critical for you to complete this next assignment on your journey toward **The Special Blessings Prayer**. You need to ask him, "*What is the very best thing about this person? What is the most noble thing this person is doing in the world?*" Without that vital piece of insider information, it will be literally impossible for you to pray the prayer effectively. *With* that information? You have the key that will unlock your own prison cell.

The rest of the items on your list are easy in comparison to this. As I've walked people through this process, I can always tell how far along in the journey they are by how convincing their response is when I ask, "What's the best thing about this person?" If they respond, "Well, she goes to church every Sunday," in a tone of voice that communicates the subtext *not that it seems to have done her any good,* then I know there's still a long way to go. But if the person bursts out with something like, "He is *such* a devoted father," with the kind of fresh enthusiasm that usually accompanies a brand new idea, then I know the blessings of God are about to chase that person down the street and overtake her.

Let me close this chapter with one final piece of advice: Please give yourself grace and time. Grace and time. Some of the wounds represented by your list are deep cuts, infected by years of fear, confusion and hate. God wants to remove all of that and I promise—I absolutely promise—he is a skilled surgeon. Oh, how I have seen him work! Indeed it has been the highest privilege of my life to walk into the surgical theatre to assist on occasion.

Grace. And time. Combine those with the courage to ask the question and wisdom to watch for the answer. Then to trust it when it comes.

Your Assignment for This Chapter: Ask God how he sees each person on your list. Be open to the possibility that God absolutely adores that person. If you can get past the shock of that revelation, maybe some of God's unlimited love will find its way into your heart.

11. Whether or Not

This was the game changer for me. Three words I did not want to hear. Three words I did not want to believe. I wanted to believe that if I prayed enough prayers, at some point, God would capitulate, as he did on behalf of the persistent widow, and give me justice against my adversaries.

And I had a lot of adversaries. Because anyone who didn't offer unconditional support for my side of every story was quickly considered an adversary.

If I were completely honest, I had the Christian version of a collection of voodoo dolls—people I prayed for all right. I prayed God would **get 'em**. That God would punish and expose them. I prayed that God would cut them down to size, prove to the whole world how horrible they were and vindicate me. Each of my prayers was like another pin in the cushion.

If I had to sum up the thrust of far too many of my prayers in one word, that one word would be **vindication.** It's what I wanted more than anything else. It's what I thought I needed. I actually thought about writing a book called ***The Prayer that Never Works*** but I knew no one would buy it. Let me urge you to resist the temptation to pray imprecatory prayers seeking revenge or vindication. I can only share my personal experience. In every case, these have backfired and in several instances, much to my shock, God vindicated the *other* person and showed me that my insecurity was the problem all along.

Now I'm finally ready to reveal the first thing God said, after I hung up the phone with the pastor's wife who told me it wasn't enough to forgive, I had to proactively bless those who'd hurt me. The answer he gave me as I wept in my rocking chair asking:

"Why on earth should I ask you to *bless* people that I want you to *punish*?"

These are the words that rocked my rocking chair and eventually rocked my world:

> *Donna, if I decide to bless someone, I'm going to bless them WHETHER OR NOT you want me to. I'm going to bless them WHETHER OR NOT you like it. I'm going to bless them WHETHER OR NOT you think it's the right thing to do.*
>
> *Your job is not to decide who is blessed and who is not. That's my job. Your job is just to agree with me.*
>
> *If I decide to bless someone, they will surely be blessed. But you will miss out on the blessings of obedience that could be yours if you stubbornly resist my command to bless those who have hurt you.*

Then I remembered: Repentance, by definition, is simply agreeing with God. That's all God was asking of me. He wasn't asking for my opinion. He didn't need my advice. Certainly not about how to deal with *his own children*. And, sad to say, almost everyone on my list was a blood-bought child of God. He was asking me to repent and come to the place where I could say these words and mean them:

> *I agree with whatever you decide, God. If you decide the best course of action here is to show the person who hurt me the same mercy and compassion extended to me at the cross, then I agree with you.*
>
> *You are God and there is no other. You are God and I am not. You alone know the full picture. So if you decide that person should be elevated to ever greater prominence and showered with every imaginable blessing, then I agree with you.*

To view it any other way is to put myself in the place of God. It's the sin of pride, declaring that I know better than God does who deserves what. That somehow I, a mere mortal, have a better grasp of the bigger picture, a deeper understanding of the souls of my fellow men, than their Creator.

That's a level of spiritual arrogance that's downright dangerous.

We don't know. We think we do. But we don't. Our Perfect Heavenly Father knows best. Let's trust him. Let's let him decide who is lifted up and who is brought low.

God happens to be very good at both. In my case, I have seen Him elevate someone *I was absolutely certain* was a complete phony and a manipulative, conniving person—all the way to the pinnacle of success in the Christian publishing and speaking industry. Guess what? God obviously didn't see her the same way I did. And sitting there with my pincushion filled with imprecatory prayers did not change his mind *at all*.

What good did it do me to seethe with bitterness and resentment—"praying" for God to expose her as a fraud and a villain—while God showered her with every human accolade and spiritual blessing imaginable?

That shouldn't be a hard question to answer: NONE.

God is also very good at bringing people low, although I haven't seen this one in my own life yet. Apparently, I'm pretty much always wrong about who the real villains are. But God is always right. In Abigail's case, Nabal was a true villain and God made sure he got exactly what was coming to him.

Just ten days after Abigail met David, it tells us:

> *The Lord struck Nabal and he died. When David heard that Nabal was dead, he said, "Praise be to the Lord, who has upheld my cause against Nabal for treating me with contempt. He has kept his servant from doing wrong and has brought Nabal's wrongdoing down on his own head." (vs. 38-39)*

So if your villain is actually a villain, God can deal with that too. My late brother Jimmy, who would have fit in extremely well with David's band of warriors, used to wear a t-shirt that said, "Kill 'em all and let God sort 'em out." I'm thinking about having a similar t-shirt made: "Love 'em all and let God sort 'em out." I'll be sure to include a link to purchase on my website; I know you'll want one of your own!

But what if Abigail had painted David as a villain too? It would have been easy to do. If someone threatened to *kill your entire family over a few sheep,* would you put them on your list of villains? You know you would!

Abigail could have wasted time praying down judgment on David's head and it wouldn't have benefited her in any way. Because the bottom line was this: Even though David sometimes lost his way along the way, God never changed his mind about David.

God never changed his mind about David. He said from the time he was a little boy, "Someday, I'm going to make you a king." God was going to bless David **whether or not** Abigail blessed him. Blaming him. Hating him. None of that would have helped Abigail in any way.

Instead, she blessed him. She agreed with God. God said, "I'm going to elevate David, make him successful, make him the king." So she simply agreed with God:

> *"And when the Lord your God has brought my master success, remember your servant." (v. 31)*

And did he remember Abigail? You better believe he did! She became his wife! And when he became the king, *she* became a queen:

> *Then David sent word to Abigail, asking her to become his wife. His servants went to Carmel and said to Abigail, "David has sent us to you to take you to become his wife."*
>
> *She bowed down with her face to the ground and said, "I am your servant and am ready to serve you and wash the feet of my lord's servants." Abigail quickly got on a donkey and, attended by her five female servants, went with David's messengers and became his wife. (vs. 39-42)*

Let that sink in.

Because she understood this simple truth, that God was going to bless David *whether or not* she got on board with it, she made the smart move and got on board. And became a queen.

Now imagine if she dug in her heels and argued with God. Imagine if she sat down with her little pincushion insisting, *"God, you've got it all wrong about David. Can't you see he's horrible? Can't you see he's a murderer? He's threatening to murder my whole family. Go get 'em, God! Punish him! Make him pay for treating us this way!"*

Do you think those so-called "prayers" would have altered David's glorious future one bit?

Absolutely not.

The only person who would have been robbed of a blessing…is Abigail. Because with that attitude, she never would have become a queen. Her destiny was to become a queen and David was the only person who could have elevated her to that position.

Oh, let that one sink in deep.

What if someone on your list—someone you are refusing to bless—is *the very person God had planned to use to elevate you into your destiny?* What if—at every turn—just as you were positioned to step into destiny, the enemy set a trap of offense between you and *the very people* who could have elevated you to the next level?

I can just about guarantee you that at least one person on your list fits into this category. In fact, the higher the call upon your life, the more likely it is that *many* people do. The enemy is strategic and one of his major goals is to thwart your destiny. An easy way for him to accomplish that mission is by causing division between you and *anyone* in a position to move you forward.

I strongly encourage you not to go on to the next chapter until God shows you who on your list this applies to. If there is any possible way to restore that relationship, you should make it a very high priority to do so.

Your assignment for this chapter is simple: Agree with God. Pray through your list one by one, disentangling your heart from any attachment to what happens to these people. If God wants to bless them to the high heavens, then so be it. Come to grips with the truth of this chapter: God is going to bless them ***WHETHER OR NOT*** you think he should. Digging in your heels and praying for God to punish them will not benefit you—and will actually do damage to you in spirit, soul and body.

Also go through your list and consider: If you were not in conflict with that person, can you see how God might have intended to use them to elevate you into your destiny?

Your Assignment for This Chapter: Add another column to your list—How might this person have been used to move me forward into my destiny?

12. Could There Be a Way Forward?

Are you ready for a test? You have to promise not to cheat. By that I mean do not look ahead to find the answer until you've given this your best shot. Please concentrate. I promise this is not some kind of a trick; it's an important exercise. Okay, here goes. I want you to read through this passage and find the two words that are noticeably absent. Two words that you would expect to find splattered all over the page considering Abigail's family is about to be murdered and she is trying desperately to save their lives:

> *"And now, my lord, as surely as the LORD your God lives and as you live, since the LORD has kept you from bloodshed and from avenging yourself with your own hands, may your enemies and all who are intent on harming my lord be like Nabal. And let this gift, which your servant has brought to my lord, be given to the men who follow you." (vs. 26-27)*

Any luck with that? Maybe this will help. The same words are also missing from this passage:

> *"No wrongdoing will be found in you as long as you live." (v. 28)*

Strangely enough, you won't find either of the words here. Crazy but true. If you haven't figured it out yet, see if the "third time's the charm" and it finally hits you:

> *"My lord will not have on his conscience the staggering burden of needless bloodshed or of having avenged himself." (v. 31)*

Here's a clue: they are probably two of your favorite words. Indeed, according to Wikipedia, one of them ranks in the Top Ten most frequently used words in the entire English language. The words, of course, are I and me.

Never once does Abigail talk about what *she* wants, what *she* thinks, what *she* needs or how *she* feels. Never once does she present this case from her perspective. Never once does she say, "*I love my kids and grandkids. I would be lost without them. I was in labor for twenty-four hours for my oldest and nearly died giving birth to the youngest. I've worked day and night for this family! How could you think of hurting me in this way. And I need the male members of my household. They are like family to me. I'm a good person. I rescue stray animals. I recycle! How could you treat me like this? Why are you doing this to ME? ME of all people. After all I've put up with in this horrible marriage, now you're going to murder my family. My life is so unfair. After everything I've done, nothing ever works out for me! Have some pity on ME.*"

By the way, the only time she uses the word "my" is when she's referring to David as "my lord." So really, there's not one thing in this entire presentation that has anything to do with everyone's three favorite people: I, Me and My.

It's almost like she got an advance copy of Dale Carnegie's *How to Win Friends and Influence People* because I couldn't help but notice how she followed his advice to the tee. I took the class two decades ago but I still remember Principle #1: Don't criticize, condemn or complain. Unless of course you *don't* want to influence people or win them to your point of view.

Up until now, that may not have seemed important to you. As far as you were concerned, *those people* are on your list and you have absolutely no desire to ever be friends with them again or to influence them in any way.

But in view of what you have likely just discovered in the previous chapter, you might want to reconsider. If there are people on your list who were in your life because God intended them to be part of your unfolding destiny—and I will absolutely *guarantee you* that is the case—maybe it's time to rethink your strategy of simply "writing them off."

What if there is a way forward? What if there's a way to bring genuine healing and reconciliation to such an extent that your relationship ends up closer than ever? Wouldn't *that* be the best possible outcome of the conflict? In the vast majority of cases, the answer is a resounding *yes*.

We know reconciliation is God's priority because the entire reason Jesus came to earth was to reconcile man to God (2 Cor. 5:19). Jesus' final prayer, his final plea, was for believers to be reconciled to one another (John 17:23). Apparently, David learned the lesson at some point because he devoted an entire psalm to the subject:

> *How good and pleasant it is*
> *when God's people live together in unity!*
>
> *It is like precious oil poured on the head,*
> *running down on the beard,*
> *running down on Aaron's beard,*
> *down on the collar of his robe.*
>
> *It is as if the dew of Hermon*
> *were falling on Mount Zion.*

> *For there the Lord bestows his blessing,*
> *even life forevermore. (Psalm 133)*

If you want the precious oil of God's anointing on your life, running down your head and seeping into your clothes so that the very fragrance of your life is beautiful and irresistible, make peace a priority. This is true for everyone, but it's especially true if you are involved in ministry. Because David got it right: God blesses his people when we choose to live in unity. And he sends extra blessings, special blessings, when we make that choice against all odds.

As always, God is a realist. So he says, "If it is possible, so far as it depends on *you,* live at peace with everyone" (Romans 12:18, emphasis added). Even God knows there are some people who are impossible to get along with. But as far as it depends on you, you should "seek peace and pursue it" (Psalm 34:14). And yes, David wrote *that* psalm, too.

In case all of those Scriptures aren't compelling enough, here's something else to ponder. When this story began, Abigail was a woman who lived with her family in David's neighborhood. But because of the grace-filled way she handled this conflict, by the end, they are closer than ever. In fact, they are husband and wife.

I don't think *anyone* could have predicted that outcome as David was hurling out death threats against her family. But God loves to do the unpredictable. Maybe he wants to do something in your life that absolutely no one could possibly predict right now. Least of all you!

But you have to cooperate with him by approaching every encounter with the same spirit of *other-focused humility* exemplified by Abigail. By the way, humility doesn't mean thinking less of yourself; it's means thinking of yourself less. Very often, the only person standing in between you and your destiny is *you*. Maybe it's time for you to get out of your own way. Maybe it's time for you to stop biting off your nose to spite your face. Maybe it's time to stop playing the *blame game* and start playing the *game of life*—and playing to win!

Maybe it's time for you to learn a few basic lessons in human relations from Abigail, who figured them out a few millennia before Dale Carnegie. If you want a biblical example of how to win friends and influence people, study this masterful encounter:

> *"The Lord your God will certainly make a lasting dynasty for my lord, because you fight the* LORD*'s battles, and no wrongdoing will be found in you as long as you live. Even though*

> *someone is pursuing you to take your life, the life of my lord will be bound securely in the bundle of the living by the* Lord *your God, but the lives of your enemies he will hurl away as from the pocket of a sling. When the* Lord *has fulfilled for my lord every good thing he promised concerning him and has appointed him ruler over Israel, my lord will not have on his conscience the staggering burden of needless bloodshed or of having avenged himself. And when the* Lord *your God has brought my lord success, remember your servant" (vs. 28-31).*

Abigail immediately reminded David what was at stake here. And it wasn't a few sheep. *It was his lasting dynasty.* She reminded him who he really was: someone who fought the Lord's battles and avoided wrongdoing. She let him know she understood the larger context of this current incident. Namely, that someone was actively pursuing him to take his life. She addressed his obvious insecurity (*only insecure people freak out when they don't immediately get what they think they need*) by reminding him that his security was in his relationship with God. She very subtly—and brilliantly—reminded him of the pinnacle of his career to date with the phrase "the pocket of a sling." This is a clear reference to his victory over Goliath.

Next, she spoke to his bright future and the promises of God concerning his destiny. She expressed absolute confidence that, no matter how bad it looked right then, she still believed in a bright future for David. She even spoke prophetically, declaring God's highest and best will for his life when she proclaimed that someday he would be ruler over Israel.

Looking at David in this scene, a single snapshot in time, *all you would see is a homeless man desperate for a few sheep*. True, that's where David was, but it's not who he was. It may have been his circumstance for a period of time, but it was never his true identity. He was born to be king. And the king he became.

Let this be a sobering reminder to us all. You have no idea who you are dealing with. That person on your list may look down and out. It may even look like God has turned his back on that person. You might be tempted to conclude, "There must be some secret sin in his life." You might even think, triumphantly, *I guess God gave her her comeuppance!*

Take care. *You might very well be dealing with a future king.*

Instead of condemning David, Abigail tried to understand him. Instead of criticizing him, which would have put him on the defensive and pushed him to justify himself, she expressed compassion. Instead of complaining about how hard this situation was on her, she put herself in his place and understood how hard this situation was on *him*.

She also understood one of the deepest human needs is the desire to feel important, which is just one of the reasons why she reminded him of his prior victories and his glorious future.

She expressed sincere admiration for his strengths while politely avoiding any mention of his weaknesses (like the public tantrum he was currently pitching). She appealed entirely to his self-interest and showed him how it was to his advantage—not *hers*—to spare her family. She understood that the only way to get anyone to do anything is to make them *want* to do it. David didn't turn around because *she wanted him to*; he made that decision because he realized it was the best option for him and he *wanted to* turn around.

Did you notice she didn't talk about *her feelings?* And she certainly didn't tell him *her feelings* were *his fault*. I'm sure she was afraid. But she didn't say so. She definitely didn't say, "YOU scared me! YOU are giving me a nervous breakdown." She left her feelings out of the discussion entirely. It wasn't about her feelings. And talking about them wouldn't have helped. It was about helping David find a way forward that made sense for him while keeping her family safe. It was about finding a win-win. Especially a win-win that let David *save face* so he could ride off feeling like he'd gotten what he came for.

What if you took the same approach to the people on your list?

What if you met them halfway and, coming from a place of deep humility, initiated a dialogue? What if rather than condemning them, you tried to genuinely understand the situation from their perspective? What if, rather than criticizing them (which never works because it *always* puts the other person on the defensive), you expressed compassion? What if, rather than complaining about how hard this situation has been on you, you put yourself in their place and tried to sincerely understand how hard this situation has been for them?

What if you expressed sincere admiration for their strengths while politely avoiding any mention of their weaknesses? What if you appealed entirely to *their* self-interest and showed them how it's to *their advantage* to resolve the conflict? What if you quit talking about *your feelings* and started talking about *the other person's destiny?*

Is it possible a conversation like that might make a difference? In some cases, the answer may be *no.*

But my guess is that, in many cases, healing could begin to take place.

Almost every situation represented on your list began with a small thing that got blown way out of proportion. That's why timing is so very important. There's a moment in every conflict when the greatest opportunity exists to defuse the situation and avoid the explosion. Abigail acted quickly and nailed the timing precisely right:

> *"Praise be to the LORD, the God of Israel, who has sent you* ***today*** *to meet me... If you had not* ***come quickly*** *to meet me, not one male belonging to Nabal would have been left alive by daybreak. (v. 32, 34, emphasis added)*

Notice: God sent her. And he sent her at exactly the right time. When God gave her marching orders, she *listened* and *acted quickly*. She didn't waste time second-guessing. She didn't try to figure it out. Good thing she didn't, because what God told her to do *didn't make any sense*. Does it make any sense to head in the direction of the person who has publicly announced he is planning to murder your entire family?

If she had *leaned on her own understanding* and tried to come up with her own alternative plan, her family would have been dead by daybreak. That's why the Bible tells us, "Trust in the Lord with all your heart and lean not on your own understanding, but in all your ways submit to him and he will make your paths straight" (Proverbs 3:5-6).

Trust God. Listen to him and when he tells you the timing is right to defuse a situation, act quickly and do exactly what he tells you to do. Very often, God will show you how to seize the moment *before* it gets completely out of hand. But since we can't turn back time, it's quite likely that the chance to defuse some situations was missed and you may have to walk through a lot of wreckage—or even a dangerous minefield—just to arrange a meeting. In those cases, before you seek peace with people, you need to seek extra wisdom from God.

Ask God to show you a specific win-win strategy that allows the *other person* a gracious way out of the mess—a strategy that allows them to save face and walk away feeling like their needs have been met. If you will do that, then you like Abigail will "go home in peace" with your words heard and your request granted (v. 35).

Your Assignment for This Chapter: Go through your list, one by one, asking God to show you: Is there a way forward in this relationship? Is there a path that might lead to reconciliation? Is it possible that I could end up closer to that person than I would have been if this conflict had never happened?

13. How Favor is Unleashed

As we saw in previous chapters, David isn't the only person in this story who ended up receiving abundantly more than he ever could have asked or imagined. All he wanted were a few sheep. Maybe some bread and water. Instead, he received an absolute feast including wine and cake. But Abigail! She was the real winner in this story, even though she never asked for anything for herself. Scratch that. My guess is that she became the real winner *precisely because* she never asked for anything for herself.

Her focus was on the kingdom. Yes, it was kingdom with a lower case, but nevertheless, her heart was to see God's plan established. Not her agenda. God's agenda. As a result, she traded a surly, mean drunk for the man after God's own heart. She went from being married to a fool to being married to a king.

How on earth is such favor from heaven unleashed upon a person's life? I am absolutely convinced of this one central truth:

Nothing unleashes the favor of God like a godly response to an unfair situation.

So if you are facing an unfair situation, that's actually very good news. In fact, the more unfair situations you face, the greater the opportunity for favor to be unleashed. But there is a big IF here. Let's be super-clear about that. Facing an unfair situation is *no guarantee* that you're going to experience an outpouring of the favor of God. In fact, the devil would love nothing more than to seize the opportunity to turn you bitter and angry. I beg you not to let him get away with it!

I read a line in a poem once that shook me to the core. It said, "A bitter old person is one of the crowning works of the devil." Write that one down and don't ever forget it. We've all met that person, haven't we? The person who talks about her bitter divorce and rancorous custody battle like it happened last week, when in fact it happened a decade ago. Or two decades ago.

You don't want to become that person. And you don't have to. If you will go through your list one more time and ask God to show you how you can respond in the most godly way possible, I'm telling you from personal experience, you will experience the favor of God in astounding ways.

Thus far, I have resisted the temptation to share a bunch of sob stories in this book. I think that strategy is working for both you and me, so I'm sticking with it. But I think it's important for me to share something with you. God told me about a decade ago,

"*You're going to lose everything, Donna. You're going to be a modern-day Job.*" If you don't believe it, don't feel bad. I didn't believe it either!

But I did lose almost everything. The first loss was a miscarriage in June of 2003. That was followed in rapid succession by a series of stunning personal and professional losses that reached into every corner of my life. The blows came in waves, just as they did for Job. And each time I told myself, *I'm sure that's the worst of it. It's all onward and upward from here.*

Then another blow would hit. When I say I lost *almost everything,* I mean it. Not one area of my life was left untouched, from health and relationships to my finances and career. I was tempted to list the losses, but what would be the point? This is about *your* list, not mine.

There were more times than I care to admit when I was like David—a crazed person marching toward Carmel desperately trying to get my needs met. But then I began pressing deeper and deeper into the power of **The Special Blessings Prayer**. I began sharing it with my online students. And as I challenged them to grab hold of this process, God challenged me to get absolutely radical in my obedience to his command:

> *Bless those who persecute you; bless and do not curse. (Romans 12:14)*

Along with that challenge, God gave me a promise. If I would force myself, through a decision of my will, to respond in a godly way no matter how unfairly I felt I was being treated, that he would pour out such blessing and favor upon my life, I wouldn't know what hit me.

Then the final blow came. A personal betrayal so utterly unexpected as to leave me reeling in shock. Something I would never have predicted in a million years from the last person on earth I thought would *ever* be unfair to me. A betrayal that pressed the *one button* in my soul that the enemy knew he could always bank on to send me into an emotional tailspin.

Instead, I fell on my face and said, "Not this time. Greater is he who is in me than he who keeps using this nonsense to destroy my life. Not this time. This time, I can do all things through Christ who strengthens me."

When I was done crying, I grabbed a notebook and filled it with page after page of every wonderful thing I could think of about that person. Then I wrote page after page of blessings, touching upon every area of that person's life. I served as the person's defense attorney and recorded myself passionately arguing that person's *version of events*. I listened to it over and over again until I believed some of it myself!

Then I picked up the phone and prayed blessing after blessing while the person wept. I prayed from my heart and meant every word. I attempted to do as Abigail had done—speaking God's highest and best, affirming all that was good in the other person and not saying one word—not one word—in defense of me, myself or I.

You may be wondering, "Did it work?" Define *work*. The relationship has not been restored, although that is my prayer and I'm convinced it would be the best possible outcome. But if "did it work" means did it *change me,* then yes, it worked beautifully. And if "did it work" means did it invite the favor of God, again, I believe the answer is yes. Absolutely yes.

Today I'm sitting here, wrapping up this book and enjoying my final days at Koro Sun Resort. I'm busily looking forward to my banana wrap massage treatment this afternoon in their spa, which was voted one of the best in the entire world. And for good reason. They don't play recordings featuring chirping birds and waterfalls. They don't need to. The birds and waterfall just outside the screened-in thatched-roof bure provide the real thing.

A few days ago, they moved me to the most beautiful villa with the best view in the entire place. I literally have the perfect location to watch *both* the sunrise *and* the sunset from my front deck overlooking the ocean. When I want to swim, I open my front door then climb down my private ladder into the warm gentle ocean. The cost of this prime location is far, far above the price I paid for a more humble abode in the rainforest section of the resort. And because I'm friends with a friend of the owner, I got a ridiculous deal on that location to begin with.

God's favor, from start to finish.

Favor is when God gives you an *unfair advantage*.

I need to say that again, because it's absolutely critical for you to "get this." If nothing else in this book has convinced you to pray blessings upon the people on your list, maybe this will. Favor is when God gives you an *unfair advantage*. And do you want to know when God feels the need to intervene in someone's life in a dramatic way? Can you guess? When someone has been treated unfairly…yet choses to respond in a godly way.

Please believe me because the words I am writing now are the truest truths I have learned in decades of walking with God. And I learned them in the crucible. If you will respond in a godly way—***if you will bless those who have spitefully used you and treated***

you unfairly—oh friend, you will gain the attention of the King upon his throne. The King who has in his power the ability to turn the heart of earthly kings. The King who commands the armies of heaven can put angels at your dispatch. The King who sees all, knows all and owns all will repay, will provide, will ASTONISH.

Do you want the intervention of the King? Do you want the King to leave his throne to personally command a legion of special forces riding to your rescue? Oh this is so easy and so obvious: pray blessings upon those who have spitefully used you. Pray like you mean it. Pray the heart of God.

Abigail went from the wife of a fool to a queen because she refused to be defeated by someone in her life who was determined to treat everyone around him unfairly.

There are a few other things I notice about Abigail that I believe invited God's favor that are worth noting and applying to our own lives.

1. Believe God rather than your circumstances

Based on circumstances, this was shaping up to be the worst day of her life. But was that true? The answer is *no*. This was the turning point and maybe the best day of her life. It was the day God set the wheels in motion to remove an evil man from her life. Based on circumstances, Abigail would have been led to believe that David was a horrible person who was going to destroy her entire family. But was that really true? Not at all. David was a godly man destined to become her husband.

Good thing she believed God, rather than her circumstances.

David was momentarily tempted to believe his circumstances, too. Based on circumstances, it looked like he was either not going to have any sheep at all, or he would have to kill to get his hands on them. Was that true? No, God had every intention of meeting David's needs that day. God, as always, had his servant's back. He had an even better plan in mind for David. Not only a feast...but a beautiful, intelligent new wife to replace the one his father-in-law had given away to another man.

As the story closes, we see both of these people got it right. Both chose to believe God rather than their circumstances. And it positioned them to experience God's favor.

2. Faithfully serve others even when your own circumstances are less than ideal

Again, we see this in both David and Abigail. David was homeless. Hardly ideal. But that didn't prevent him from faithfully serving the local rich guy. Rather than being jealous of someone else's blessings and sitting around feeling sorry for himself (as we are often tempted to do), he served. And as a result, God eventually gave David riches far beyond anything Nabal could have fathomed.

We've already looked extensively at how Abigail resisted the temptation to focus on her own needs and faithfully served David and his men by serving them a fabulous feast.

When we're going through tough times, one of the toughest things to do is go help someone else. And because God *knows* it's a tough thing to do, he honors and rewards those who are willing to do it. He releases his favor.

3. Be diligent to develop your gifts in obscurity

One thing almost every one of God's choicest servants in the Bible have in common is their determination to be diligent to develop their gifts in obscurity. David developed skill with a slingshot sitting around in the middle of nowhere, even though his family obviously didn't appreciate him. It was precisely that skill that God used to position him for an outpouring of favor.

Abigail developed skill in running a household, although I sincerely doubt she ever received a drop of appreciation from her surly, mean husband. And again, it was precisely that skill (the ability to mobilize her staff to quickly throw together a feast) that positioned her for favor.

Few things in life feel more unfair than using your gifts when it seems no one appreciates you. Guess what? The *less appreciated* you are, the better! Keep developing that skill and one day, I promise you this, God will use *that exact skill* to position you to receive favor.

4. Seize your moment when it finally comes

David did not hesitate for a second when his moment arrived. He stepped up to the plate and took down the giant. The rest is history. Abigail didn't hesitate either. The minute she heard that an army of angry, hungry men were coming against her, she knew exactly what to do. In her own way, she took down a giant that day. And she did it with style.

Speaking of seizing the moment. Did you notice that the *instant* David heard that Abigail's husband had died, he issued the marriage proposal?

Your moment is coming, I promise you that! When it does, do not shrink back. Do not hesitate. Seize your moment. And experience your own outpouring of God's favor!

May this be true of all of us: "But we do not belong to those who shrink back and are destroyed, but to those who have faith" (Hebrews 10:39).

Your Assignment for This Chapter: Rejoice that the unfair treatment you've received from the people on your list has perfectly positioned you to experience the favor of God.

14. How To Get the Most Out of the Prayer

In the next chapter, you will read the words to **The Special Blessings Prayer**. Having done all of the foundational work leading up to this point, I'm confident this is going to be a powerful experience for you. But before we get there, I'd like to give you seven very practical steps you can take that literally have the potential to unleash atomic spiritual power into your life.

These principles apply at any time during your journey with God, but are particularly potent as preparation for this prayer.

Step 1: Get Desperate for God

There are two ways to get to Step 1. The first is voluntary. We make the choice and come to God in humility. We allow the Holy Spirit to hold the mirror of truth before us and when we do, we will automatically find ourselves in a place of absolute desperation when we see the massive chasm between God's standard and our reality, between who God is calling us to become and how we are currently living.

I suspect that, for many people, facing that list day after day has accomplished Step 1 quite effectively. You know, perhaps more clearly than ever before, that it's time to release these old debts. But you sense that without a mighty move of God in your heart, you're incapable of doing it.

The other way is involuntary. That's when God loves us so much He arranges circumstances to get our attention.

When David finally came to his senses in this scene and realized how close he came to doing something he would have regretted for the rest of his life, God had his heart right where he wanted it: humble and contrite.

It may very well be that you picked up this book in the first place because that's where you're at right now. If so, I actually think that's a good sign. God will only ever reveal what he is ready to heal. This is your time.

Step 2. Declare a Fast

Okay, so not many people will tell this to you straight. There *is* a secret. *A powerful spiritual secret.* One believers throughout church history have known full well. But since it makes the vast majority of contemporary Christians extremely uncomfortable, the enemy has done a masterful job of labeling anyone who attempts to let the secret out of the bag a Pharisee. And as he always does, he takes Scripture out of context to effectively hoodwink millions of believers.

In my personal walk with God, and in helping thousands worldwide to grow in their faith, I've found fasting to be the single most effective tool for inviting the presence of God. And in the presence of God, the possibility for miracles always exists.

It's beyond the scope of this book to do a full-blown teaching on fasting. I offer an online class, 30 Days In The Presence of God's Power, that includes extensive training and times of corporate fasting. Believers from six continents have experienced tremendous answers to prayer and I would encourage you to learn more about it on my website. For now, let me simply suggest that you prayerfully consider a minimum fast of three days; ideally ten would be better, especially if you have practiced the spiritual discipline of fasting regularly in the past.

It's important to understand that praying **The Special Blessings Prayer** is also a process itself. I'll say more about that when we get to the prayer. There are people on your list you will likely have to pray over for many hours, days, weeks and even months before you know you've broken through to the other side of your pain. The surest way to shorten that time frame is fasting.

So if you'd rather get your spiritual breakthrough quickly and be free of the pain connected to the people on your list, the solution is fasting before and during your season of prayer. I always encourage my online students to fast and pray for ten days when they first encounter **The Special Blessings Prayer**. Perhaps three days before beginning and then seven days of focused prayer with fasting. Fasting gets God's attention. It also stills your soul in a way that allows your spirit to soar. I don't know any other way to explain it; I just know *it works*! So remember:

The Special Blessings Prayer + Fasting = Atomic Power for Spiritual Breakthrough

Step 3. Determine What *Has to Go* to Make Room for This Process

To make the most of this spiritual experience, some of your normal routine is going to have to be put to the side for awhile. You will need to proactively make room in your life for God to work in a special way. You're not going to be able to squeeze it into your already hectic schedule. That just won't work.

What *has to go* is actually different for different people. But typically, it's some seemingly harmless habit you've developed like watching the news, reading a novel before bed, online activities and so on. Often, we are tripped up in our spiritual walk, not by "bad" things, but by a never-ending barrage of "not-too-bad," "no-big-deal," "I'm-sure-God-doesn't-mind" things. If the devil came to you to suggest you rob a bank, you'd say NO WAY. So he comes with endless hours of distractions instead.

So think about your daily routine. You are looking for an activity that *kills* an hour a day. Remove that activity and use that same time to focus on **The Special Blessings Prayer**. Then rather than *killing time,* you can begin *redeeming time*.

Step 4: Embrace the Initially Uncomfortable Experience of Absolute Silence

One of my favorite verses is Isaiah 30:15 (NLT), "*In quietness and confidence shall be your strength.*" There is an incredible strength that comes through quiet. Through solitude and silence. This, again, is something lost on the contemporary church. Even our church services are typically filled with noise. Never a moment of absolute quiet. In fact, when I try to create quiet at events where I'm speaking, the crowd gets nervous and restless after about a minute. No exaggeration. No wonder we are weak and exhausted. Something precious has been lost.

I'll never forget the first time I experienced this ancient spiritual discipline, still practiced by many of the oldest denominations around the world. But it's quite out of fashion in most churches today. I stayed at a monastery for a four-day silent retreat. No words were spoken. When it was time for meals, one of the monks rang a bell and we all gathered.

At first your mind is racing a million miles a minute. Then you suspect you might be going crazy. But eventually, you begin to rest in the silence. Silence means intentionally quieting both outer and inner voices. And it's so very empowering.

> *"Stand at the crossroads and look; ask for the ancient paths, ask where the good way is, and walk in it, and you will find rest for your souls." (Jeremiah 6:16)*

The ancient path is the path of quiet. So turn off the noise. Turn off all the electronic devices. Yes. All of them. Even turn off the music. Turn off your own thoughts…harder than it sounds, by the way! But it gets easier with practice. Just be quiet for a season. Listen for that still, small voice. God has wonderful things to say to you and about you. When you turn off the rest of the noise, you will hear. And when you hear what God has to say to you and about you, you'll be so fired up, you'll become unstoppable!

There are few things on earth more empowering than a sure word from God. Just ask David! Why do you think he responded so quickly to Abigail's words? Because she was simply repeating what God had already spoken to him in quiet moments of worship and contemplation among the sheep pastures of ancient Israel:

> *"The Lord your God will certainly make a lasting dynasty for my lord, because you fight the Lord's battles." (v. 28)*

> *"When the Lord has fulfilled for my lord every good thing he promised concerning him and has appointed him ruler over Israel." (v. 30)*

I can't even tell you how many hardships and valleys I have been able to endure just by clinging to a ***sure word*** God gave me back in July 1980. One night under a moonlit sky as I stood alone beside the Delaware River, God clearly said, "I'm going to take you all over the world and use you in a mighty way for my Kingdom." Nothing and no one could take that promise from me. And oh, how my spirit came to attention whenever someone *confirmed* that word, usually at the very moment when I was ready to give up.

I wonder what amazing thing God would whisper to you in the silence? You'll never know until you turn off the noise.

Begin with fifteen minutes a day of absolute silence before God. Don't listen to worship music. Don't read anything. Don't talk. Don't even "pray" if praying means you are doing the talking. Just LISTEN. Always do this *before* you spend time pressing into **The Special Blessings Prayer**. What a difference it will make!

If you are ready for a challenge, consider a silent retreat. Go away to a quiet place to rest and listen more intently. Many convents and monasteries around the world will open up to visitors for this purpose. If you have a long list, *a retreat to advance* may be the shortest path to freedom.

Step 5: Pray in a New Way

This, for me, is one of the most powerful of the seven steps. And it's small and simple to do. It doesn't have to be complicated or difficult; it just has to be effective. Here's what I mean: whatever prayer position you usually adopt (whether sitting, standing, kneeling and so on), try something different.

I always loved to pray in my rocking chair. My prayer chair. My favorite spot. But when I got absolutely desperate one day, I got up out of that chair and got flat on my back on the hardwood floor. The difference was instant and incredible. Something about *not* trying to make myself cozy and comfortable caused a spiritual shift to happen.

Of course, one very practical reason this new position worked for me is that I could keep my eyes open without being distracted by anything around me.

Maybe it's just me, but I prefer to pray with my eyes open. A pastor friend once pointed out to me, "The only time the Bible records Jesus closing his eyes was when his work was finished on the cross. In every other case when he prayed, it says he looked up or that he lifted up his eyes." When I'm flat on my back, it's just easier to look up and lift up my eyes.

My daughter Taraneh stood on the night watch at IHOP, the International House of Prayer in Kansas City, from midnight to 6:00 a.m. for six straight months. And when I say she stood, I mean she literally stood all night. She took Psalm 134:1 (NKJV) to heart: "Bless the LORD, all you servants of the LORD, who stand by night in the house of the LORD!" She said it helped her to stay focused and prevented her mind from drifting.

I'm not saying you have to pray flat on your back on a hardwood floor (although I highly recommend it). Or that you should stand and pray for six straight hours every night (although I'm sure that would be amazing!). I'm saying no matter what you are doing right now, it's time to shake things up a little. Pray differently. On purpose. If you usually sit, try standing. If you usually stand, try walking. If you usually walk, try kneeling. Try something radically different that signals to your body: *Something new is happening here. We're taking this to another level.*

Step 6: Just Agree with God

I was a pre-law major in college. And anyone who knows me will tell you, if I hadn't been called into full-time ministry, I would have been a *great* lawyer. Because I can argue with anyone about anything, with or without information. As I've already admitted, most of my so-called prayer time was spent "advocating my case." Telling God what was wrong with everyone and everything around me.

That's why I was astonished how powerful the internal shift was when I finally stopped arguing with God. Stopped explaining to Him why *everyone else* was the problem. Oh the freedom, the release, the tears of joy when I finally came to the place where I could ***just agree with him***.

When God says, "Do everything without complaining or arguing" in Philippians 2:14, believe it or not, *he thought we'd understand that prayer falls under the category of "everything."* Fortunately, there are alternative ways to pray. Jesus gave us the example in the Lord's Prayer. The disciples came to Jesus and said, "We notice that when *you* pray, power is unleashed. How can we pray like THAT?" And before he gave them the Lord's Prayer, he told them the secret. The secret that holds the key to effective prayer—the key to unleashing God's power when we pray. He said,

"Your father knows what you need before you ask him" (Matthew 6:8).

Think about how much wasted time Jesus just saved us. We don't have to waste our prayer time telling God what we want and what we think we need. He's already got that figured out. He already knows what we really need and it's often not what we think we need. And as we saw in the example of David, God is more than capable of delivering above and beyond anything we might ask or imagine. David thought he needed sheep. God thought he deserved sheep, bread, wine, cakes…and a fabulous new wife!

This profound truth frees us to forget about ourselves and concentrate on something larger. "Thy Kingdom come…Thy will be done." It liberates us from wasting time pleading with God or arguing with God. And positions us to get into agreement and alignment with what God has already decided. He has already decided WHETHER OR NOT he's going to bless the people on your list. It's time to adopt a permanent new attitude in prayer of simply agreeing with God.

Step 7: Let Go of All the Stupid Stuff

When David finally let go of his demands for some stupid sheep from Nabal, it positioned him to receive what God had in mind to give him.

I want to share a major turning point in my life with you. The exact moment when I decided to stop arguing with God. Stopped defending myself to God. Stopped demanding things from God and just listened to Him for a change and agreed with whatever He said.

In the two weeks leading up to a mission trip where I was scheduled to speak thirteen times in seven days, I had been following the steps I've shared with you so far and praying through my Special Blessings List. Being quiet and waiting and listening for God to speak. God began to do this really wild thing. He began to show me my life. It was almost like watching a movie screen where God would show me one scenario after another where I blew it. Where I sinned. (Sinning is just missing the mark.) He would show me an attitude. "*You were unloving, Donna. You were impatient here. You lacked self-control. You weren't faithful. You didn't deal with that person gently.*"

There was no condemnation. *There is no condemnation for those who are in Christ*. It wasn't about God beating me up and telling me I was a loser. I'm in charge of that. Me and the devil. We've got that covered so God doesn't need to do that!

God gave me an incredible gift: seeing my life through HIS eyes. As we watched together, he would gently say things like, "*See, daughter. That harsh edge there, that cutting sarcasm? Daughter, that's what's holding you back.*" In many cases, God was showing me interactions with people from my Special Blessings List. He was helping me to see my part in the whole sorry mess.

Less than twenty-four hours before my flight departed for the mission trip, the moment that would change everything happened. I will never recover from this moment. God said to me, "*So daughter, do you remember the water bottle?*" And I knew exactly what scene He was going to play. I knew!

And sure enough, He started playing the scene.

I'd been invited to speak at a retreat in California up in the high desert. I arrived a day early because I like to get there and get situated. The church staff who were hosting me asked, "Do you need anything, Donna?" And me—being the humble, easy-to-please servant of God that I am—did not provide them with a long list of demands. Quite the contrary. I said, "Thank you so much for asking! Don't worry, though, I don't need caviar, don't need lobster, don't need anybody to entertain and amuse me. Please don't take me shopping or sightseeing. But actually, I do dehydrate very rapidly so the only thing I need is a case of water. I'm a fish! I'm going to blow through that water. So could you please, pretty please—ASAP—bring me a case of water?"

That was Thursday. But Thursday came and went: no water. Friday, the event began: still no water delivered to my room. Friday night, I taught my little heart out and then prayed for the women until two in the morning. I went back to my room: still no water. Saturday morning, afternoon, evening: still no water!

Finally it was to the point that whenever I wasn't teaching, praying, doing what I had to do, I was thinking, "*Can you believe it? Can you believe these people can't give me a stinkin' case of water bottles?*"

I didn't have a car so I couldn't go get water. I know you have compassion, so you're probably thinking: "*I would never treat Donna Partow like that. Those horrible people.*"

And that's the way I saw it too. In fact, I'm pretty sure I uttered the Four Words of Doom at some point that weekend: After Everything I've Done! All I wanted was a few sheep…oh, wait. That was David. But really, isn't it exactly the same thing? I felt I was owed something and they had withheld it.

Anyway, when God said, "*Daughter, do you remember about the water bottle?*" I knew exactly what He meant. So I said, "*Oh, Lord. I know, I agree with you. I am definitely one of your best vessels out there. I see how I just suffer for you.*"

To which God responded, "*That's not what I was getting at.*"

And I broke.

I wept so hard my face hurt. I wept for four solid hours, grieving and weeping because I knew in that moment that I had let something as utterly ridiculous as a lousy water bottle stand in between me and my destiny. That water bottle was exactly the kind of stupid stuff that stood between me and the woman of God I could be—full of love, walking in his favor and power. More to the point, it was *exactly the kind of thing* that created the rifts that landed people on my Special Blessings List in the first place.

Now don't get me wrong. I never once during this process felt that God was angry. I felt full assurance of his love for me. He was simply holding the mirror of truth before me, saying, "*Daughter, you asked me to show you why you aren't experiencing my power and favor. Why you aren't walking in the full anointing and authority that's available to you. Why you aren't the kind of woman who walks into a situation and it has to bend the knee to me. It's stupid stuff like this. It's you wanting a lousy water bottle. If you were really that thirsty, you could have had water from the kitchen sink. Or even the toilet, for that matter. Stop being so determined to get your way."*

My friend, this is the final step and the most critical one as you prepare to actually pray the prayer. Ask God to show you anything that is preventing you from experiencing his love, favor and power.

And no matter what he shows you, no matter how small or large, just agree with him. Even if you are absolutely certain that *you* are not the problem, that you are absolutely 100 percent in the right. Just agree with him. There's no better position for your heart to be in than *that place of humble brokenness before God* as you turn the page—both literally and metaphorically.

Your Assignment for This Chapter: Add one final column and ask God to show you "What was my part in the whole sorry mess?"

15. This Prayer Won't Do You Any Good

To tell you otherwise would be the equivalent of spiritual malpractice. You deserve nothing but the truth from me, so here it is. This prayer won't do you any good whatsoever unless you walk through the process first. That means not just *reading* this book in its entirety; it means *working through* the material.

Otherwise, this prayer will not only be of no benefit, it might actually do you harm. How? Because it won't "work" and you'll walk away disillusioned by what feels like one more pie-in-the-sky promise for the life you're dreaming of. You'll walk away from the one resource that has been *proven to dramatically and permanently change people's lives* to continue searching for answers that aren't there to find.

Let me give you an analogy. You and your best friend were born with the same crippling hip ailment. You have both spent your lives in constant pain, walking with an embarrassing limp. It's actually been a bond between the two of you all these years. Then your friend finds a specialist, goes through a treatment program and wakes up from surgery completely healed. No more pain. No more limp.

At first, you're skeptical. You've tried it all and nothing lasts. But months pass and your friend is feeling terrific. She's out riding bikes, hiking hills, strolling on the beach with a big smile on her face—all the things you've always dreamed of doing, but can't. Finally, you decide to go for it.

You make an appointment with the specialist. The big day arrives, you sit down in the office and say, "Doctor, I'd like you to wake me up from surgery."

The doctor seems confused. "What do you mean?"

"Well," you explain, "my best friend had the same crippling hip ailment I was born with. She said that when you woke her up from surgery, she was completely healed. And she's out there living a great life now. Honestly, I'm starting to feel a little jealous. Like I've been left behind. I'm missing out. So I'd like you to wake me up from surgery."

"I see," says the doctor. "Unfortunately, I think you have misunderstood. Waking her up from surgery is not what healed her. There was a series of procedures leading up to the surgery, there was pre-op, the operation and the post-op recovery. Waking up from the surgery is not the secret in the sauce."

"No, doctor, ***you*** don't understand," you counter, getting a little testy. "I don't want or need any of those other things! I've heard about them for years. And in fact, I've tried surgery before. It doesn't work. My friend said, and I quote, 'When I woke up from surgery, I was healed.' So that's what I want and nothing else. Can you do it or not?"

The obvious answer is NO!

The secret in the sauce here is not words in a prayer. This isn't a lucky charm. It's not a rabbit's foot. It's not a miracle medallion. The power is in the preparation process. This is not an intellectual exercise; it's a spiritual one. It's not about what you know in your head; it's about what the Holy Spirit wants to do in your heart.

So if you've turned to this page, planning to pray the prayer and unleash God's love, favor and power upon your life, you're going to be very disappointed if you proceed any further. I can predict right now what will happen. You'll scan through it, notice it appears to be primarily about forgiveness and think:

> Really? That's what she's got? Seriously? The old forgiveness thing? Please, Donna. I've heard a million sermons on that. I get it. Yada, yada. Blah, blah, blah. I'm sure there are people who need to forgive and well, maybe there are a couple people I should probably forgive. But guess what? They haven't *asked for* my forgiveness, they *don't deserve* my forgiveness and it's just not a priority for me. I cut that person out of my life long ago,

anyway. In fact, I'm pretty sure they are reprobate and God himself is finished with them. So, it's a non-issue.

What I need is Special Blessings from God. What I need is what I thought you were promising when I bought this book. (Right now, I'm thinking about writing a *strongly worded letter* to request a refund.) What I need is God's power and especially his favor. The love doesn't sound too bad, either. Especially if you mean someone to love me and treat me right. Now *that? That* I would be interested in!

But this? This just looks like some pre-packaged prayer about forgiveness. And that's not what I need it all. And to be completely honest, I'm absolutely convinced that when God's love, favor and power are unleashed upon my life, it'll be a whole lot easier to forgive anyway. When God gives me a million dollars, don't you think it'll be a piece of cake to "forgive my debtors"—like my in-laws who cheated me out of $50,000? When God gives me a promotion, trust me, it will be no sweat to forgive those lying conniving co-workers who cost me that regional manager position. When God sends me a new love, a wonderful spouse who adores me, you can be

> sure I'll happily forgive my ex for cheating on me with my best friend.
>
> So Donna, unless there's a prayer I can plainly see shows me how to get those things—the things I really need—then I think I should just put this book down and do something else.

What makes me so sure that's what your reaction will be if you skip the book and just read the prayer? Because I wrote exactly what I would be tempted to think if I hadn't experienced the power of this prayer. After thirty years in ministry on six continents, if there's one thing I've learned it's this: Deep in our heart of hearts, we're all pretty much the same.

So here's what I need you to do if you "skipped to the prayer." Don't read it. Seriously. Please don't. Go back to page one and work through this book. And I'll see you back here, where I'll be anxiously waiting to *wake you up from surgery*.

If you have worked through the book and have your list ready, you may proceed with the prayer.

Dear Lord,

If you desire to bless ____________ you will do so whether or not I pray for him/her. But you will not bless me unless I obey your command to bless those who have cursed (thought or spoken ill of me) or hurt me.

Therefore, by faith, I choose to bless ____________. I cancel the debt s/he owed me to ____________________________. I declare that s/he owes me absolutely nothing.

If s/he cheated me out of anything—whether love, opportunity, money or any other blessing, including ____________________________—I believe you will give me double for my trouble. You will repay me in full and much more. So I release them from the debt.

Besides, I now realize I could have responded differently by ___________________________________ and had a very different outcome.

I see that s/he is doing noble things in the area of _______________. I ask you to bless him/her. I look forward to reaping the blessing I've just sown.

Thank you for setting me free from the curse of unforgiveness. Right now, in the name of Jesus, I declare that the blood of Jesus covers over the offense and all the sin that resulted. I hereby reclaim any ground given over to the enemy by my sinful response and I slam the door on his ability to wreak havoc in my life because of it. I declare that greater is he who is in me than he who has used this garbage to gain access to my life. This sin cannot be used against me from this day forward.

I am free.
Amen.

Remember, praying this prayer once will not work like a magic wand to heal all of your relationships and open the floodgates of heaven. Instead, today you have began the second part of your journey. The first part was learning the *why* behind each element of the prayer; the second part is the most difficult process of *walking it out* until the breakthrough comes.

How will you know? There are two surefire ways to know for sure: the first one is much easier to pass. You hear that something *bad* happened to someone on your list and you are genuinely sad. That's progress worth celebrating. The second will take much longer, but it will happen. You hear something *wonderful* happened to someone on your list and you are truly happy. When you can obey the mandate to grieve with those who grieve and rejoice with those who rejoice even when the "those" in question are people you once considered enemies, you are walking in a level of emotional wholeness and spiritual maturity most people will never experience.

You will be walking in God's love, favor and power to such a degree that your entire life is a Special Blessing—to you and to everyone you meet.

Thank You!

I hope you've enjoyed The Special Blessings Prayer and you're armed with more answers to help you do and become all God has destined for your life!

With the quick links below you'll be able to rate this book, Tweet, and share about it on Facebook. Please take a moment to do that. I'd be very grateful and it will help others who need clarity about how to unleash God's love, favor and power in their own lives.

I'd also appreciate it very much if you could leave a short review of the book on Amazon via the link below. It will help me improve this and future books and help other believers like yourself decide if The Special Blessings Prayer has the answers they are looking for.

Love & Prayers
~ Donna

P.S. Be sure to take the next steps:

Claim your Special Blessings gifts: www.specialblessingsprayer.com/gift

Share your prayer requests with me on Facebook: www.facebook.com/donnapartow

About The Author

Donna Partow is an international best-selling author whose books have sold more than a million copies worldwide. Her uncommon transparency and passion for Christ have been used by God in ministry on six continents.

Whether she's speaking in a mud hut in Mozambique, a street corner in Peru, a missionary conference in Papua New Guinea, or at the CIA headquarters, her mission is to empower her listeners to go to the next level in their destiny.

Donna is a full-time missionary who makes her home wherever her head hits the pillow. Her primary teaching platform today is the internet. More than 20,000 people have studied with her online.

You can stay updated about her upcoming classes, and receive a free copy of her book, **Becoming the Ultimate You**, by visiting www.donnapartow.org/ultimate

Made in the USA
Columbia, SC
12 July 2019